THE ACTS OF PETER

Early Christian & Apocrypha

Julian V. Hills

Harold W. Attridge

Dennis R. MacDonald

THE ACTS OF PETER

Robert F. Stoops, Jr.

Edited by Julian V. Hills

POLEBRIDGE PRESS
Salem, Oregon

Cover and interior design and production by Robaire Ream

Library of Congress Cataloging-in-Publication Data

Acts of Peter. English.
  The Acts of Peter / [translated by] Robert F. Stoops, Jr. ; edited by Julian V. Hills.
     p. cm. -- (Early Christian apocrypha ; v. 4)
  Includes bibliographical references (p.   ) and indexes.
  ISBN 978-1-59815-022-3 (alk. paper)
  I. Stoops, Robert Franklin. II. Hills, Julian Victor. III. Title.
  BS2880.P47A3 2012
  229'.925--dc23

                                                              2012017546

CONTENTS

SERIES PREFACE

The series *Early Christian Apocrypha &* (*ECA&*), the first such publication by north American scholars, is designed as a study edition of early Christian apocryphal texts and related writings. These comprise the standard set of New Testament apocrypha (gospels, acts, epistles, apocalypses) along with other, some less well known, writings that emerged from the early Christian movement, such as homiletical, polemical, exegetical, and church order tracts. Writings reckoned "orthodox" and "heretical" by contemporaries and later authorities will be included.

The publisher and the editors have had several goals in mind. First, to provide quotable and lively renderings into modern U.S. English—satisfying both to the specialist and to the non-expert reader. Second, to offer full introductions and bibliographies that will situate the texts in question in their larger Christian and Greco-Roman contexts. Third, to supply brief commentary explaining technical aspects of the writing and the movement of the text—storyline or theological argument. Fourth, to add "verse numbers" where previous editions gave only larger section or chapter numbers.

Where appropriate, the texts will be annotated with cross-references, not only within the biblical canon but also outside it—in due course supplying a network of interconnected references to assist comparative study. A full index of texts, biblical and non-biblical, will conclude each volume.

SIGLA, ABBREVIATIONS, CONVENTIONS

Aaa	Lipsius-Bonnet, *Acta apostolorum apocrypha*
AcPetBG	*Acts of Peter, Berlin Coptic Codex* (BG 8502,4 128–141.7)
AcPetVerc	*Acts of Peter, Actus Vercellenses*
AcPetMart	*Acts of Peter, Martyrdom*
BAGD	Bauer-Arndt-Gingrich-Danker, *Greek-English Lexicon*
LPGL	Lampe, *Patristic Greek Lexicon*
LS	Lewis and Short, *A Latin Dictionary*
LSJ	Liddell Scott Jones, *Greek-English Lexicon*
NHC	Nag Hammadi Codex, followed by codex and line number

<and>	words supplied *ad sensum*
[then]	words supplied to fill whole or partial *lacunae* (gaps)
»	indicates the place where the principal reference list of passages related by a common theme or expression is to be found

INTRODUCTION

The *Acts of Peter* is a Christian entry in the second-century marketplace of competing religious claims. The surviving portions deal primarily with the conflict between the apostle Peter and Simon Magus in Rome and the apostle's martyrdom. It employs both traditional stories and the literary conventions of its day in a free manner in order to assure believers that they have ample reason to remain loyal to Christ, or return to faith if they have faltered. Simon is presented as a deceiver, whose false claims and false miracles initially seduce the crowds in Rome, including most of the Christians. Peter, and to a lesser extent Paul, are presented as examples of believers who have arrived at secure faith after either weakness or enmity. The apostles are not presented as divine men but as channels for the power of God or Christ (Poupon, 1981; Kaestli and Junod, 1983: 683; Achtemeier, 1976: 170–75). Although the author certainly values the spiritual realm above the physical, the *Acts of Peter* is neither as dualistic nor as rigorously ascetic as many of the other New Testament apocrypha with which it shares narrative patterns and theological motifs.

As is often the case with literature of this type, no complete copy has survived. Although the *Acts of Peter* was composed in Greek, most of its contents have survived only in a single manuscript of a Latin translation, the *Actus Vercellenses* (V). This version of the *Acts of Peter* begins with Paul's departure from Rome to minister to the people of Spain. Shortly after Paul's departure, Simon Magus appears in Rome and seduces the masses, along with most of the Christians, by means of his wonders. In response, Christ appears to Peter in Jerusalem and directs him to set sail for Rome to counter the works of Simon. Once in Rome, Peter preaches and performs numerous miracles for the benefit of both believers and unbelievers. He also confronts Simon in wide-ranging public debates. Simon gives voice to various challenges faced by Christians in the second century. At times he denounces Jesus on the grounds of his obscurity and the ignominy of his death. At other times Simon claims that he reveals a superior god. Peter responds with arguments that include the fulfillment of prophecy, the miracles worked by Jesus during his earthly career, and the mighty works that God/Christ is now accomplishing through his apostle.

The conflict quickly develops into a contest of miracles. In the first public competition, Simon kills a young man with the power of his words. Peter exposes Simon's deceits by raising not only that man from the dead, but two others as well. Both are sons of widows, one rich the other poor. Thus, Christ's power is shown to be available to all. A second public confrontation takes place when Simon attempts to demonstrate his divine nature by flying. He is brought down by Peter's prayer and dies of his injuries a few days later. Peter's victory over Simon documents the superiority of the benefits, both material and spiritual, that Christ offers to those who are loyal to him.

A subplot around the senator Marcellus amplifies the theme of reliance on Christ by exposing the spiritual weakness of a human patron. Although wealthy believers—and even nonbelievers—are obligated to support poor believers, they are repeatedly shown to be unworthy as spiritual leaders (Stoops, 1986, 1991; Perkins, 2009). Independent episodes, such as those dealing with Peter's daughter, Rufina, the fish, and Chryse, reinforce and elaborate the themes found in the main storyline.

The text ends with Peter's martyrdom at the hands of the prefect Agrippa, whose concubines refuse to share his bed after being converted by Peter. When Agrippa's intentions are discovered, Peter is persuaded to leave the city. When he does, he encounters Christ approaching the city and asks the famous question: "Lord, where are you going?" Christ answers that he is coming "to be crucified again," which Peter recognizes as a reference to his own impeding martyrdom. Christ returns to heaven, and the apostle cheerfully turns back into the city. Before his execution Peter explains the mystical meaning of the cross and then asks to be crucified head downward. From the cross he gives a second, longer speech interpreting his inverted position as a sign of conversion and repentance. After the apostle's death, Nero has a vision which causes him to end his persecution of the believers in Rome.

Debate continues as to whether the material dealing with Paul in the opening chapters, and the final chapter, which introduces Nero, belonged to the earliest versions of the *Acts of Peter*. The relationship between the Latin version and the short texts preserved elsewhere dealing with Peter's daughter, and the daughter of a gardener, is also not fully established. The fact that the same concerns appear consistently throughout the *Acts of Peter* and these additional stories argues for the integrity of the text as reconstructed. However, any interpretation of the *Acts of Peter* must keep in mind that uncertainties remain concerning the reconstruction, that most of the material survives only in later translations, and that even the Greek manuscripts are abridgements made for different purposes.

IDENTITY AND
EXTERNAL EVIDENCE

The *Acts of Peter* is often grouped with four similar early Christian texts from the second and third centuries: the *Acts of John*, *Acts of Paul*, *Acts of Thomas* and *Acts of Andrew*. The grouping derives from an entry in Photios's *Bibliotheka* (cod. 114). Photios, the patriarch of Constantinople from 858 to 861 and again from 878 to 886 C.E., indicates that he produced his catalogue of books from memory. Photios describes the five works as belonging to a single volume, *The Travels (Periodoi) of the Apostles*, and attributes the entire collection to Leucius Charinos. Although the five texts are clearly related, the differences among them make it clear that they are not the work of a single author. The titles given to apocryphal acts and many other noncanonical writings were descriptive of their content and were not fixed. Photios uses the title *Acts of Peter (Praxeis Petrou)* to refer to versions of the Pseudo-Clementine romances (cod. 113), but he may have known manuscripts which attached the text now known as the *Acts of Peter* to the *Recognitions* (Baldwin, 2005: 170–74).

The earliest explicit reference to the *Acts of Peter* appears in Eusebius's *Ecclesiastical History* 3.3.2. Eusebius rejects the *Acts of Peter (Praxeis Petrou)* along with the *Preaching of Peter (Kerygma Petrou)*, the *Gospel of Peter (Euangelion Petrou)* and the *Revelation of Peter (Apokalypsis Petrou)*. As with the other apocryphal acts, he argues that the *Acts of Peter* is not cited by earlier Christian writers. However, a little earlier Eusebius quotes a passage from Origen's commentary *On Genesis* describing Peter's activity in Asia Minor, his inverted crucifixion in Rome, and Paul's martyrdom under Nero after his activity in Illyria (*Hist. eccl.* 3.1.2). It is very likely that Origen found this information in the *Acts of Peter* (Poupon, 1998), although some scholars reject this conclusion (Schneemelcher, 1989: 272; 1992: 273; Baldwin, 2005: 76).

WITNESSES TO THE TEXT

From the beginning of the eighteenth century through most of the nineteenth century, discussions of the *Acts of Peter* were based on attempts to reconstruct an "original" version by combining elements of the *Preaching of Peter (Kerygma Petrou)*, known primarily through quotations in Clement of Alexandria and Origen (text and commentary in Cambe, 2003), with material from the Pseudo-Clementine romances, especially the hypothetical basic document or *Grundschrift* (Jones, 1982: 8–20), and the Pseudo-Linus *Passion of Peter*. Portions of Pseudo-Abdias, and the Pseudo-Marcellus *Acts of Peter and Paul*, were also used by some. This phase of scholarship is conveniently summarized by Matthew Baldwin (2005: 30–38).

Everything changed with Richard Adelbert Lipsius's publication of a new edition of apocryphal acts in 1891. His *Acts of Peter and Simon (Actus Petri <cum> Simone)* was based on the Latin *Actus Vercellenses,* which offered a continuous narration of the confrontation between Peter and Simon in Rome followed by the martyrdom of Peter. Lipsius also made use of two Greek manuscripts of the *Martyrdom of Peter* drawn from a source apparently very close to the Greek behind the Vercelli martyrdom. This martyrdom includes both the *Quo vadis* scene and Peter's crucifixion in a head downward position. It quickly became clear that the new text represented an important source for many of the texts that researchers previously relied on to reconstruct the *Acts of*

Peter. Lipsius argued that the Vercelli version is an orthodox revision of an earlier gnostic form of the *Acts of Peter*, which is better represented by the Pseudo-Linus *Passion of Peter* (Lipsius, 1891: 2/1. 109–42). However, his needlessly complex reconstruction of the text's history has never found wide acceptance. The division between gnostic (or "Gnostic," if referring to developed metaphysical systems) and orthodox theologoumena no longer seems as clear as Lipsius believed, especially in non-canonical writings aimed at a broad audience and incorporating a variety of materials (Schneemelcher, 1992: 280–82). Lispsius's text, as further emended and supplemented by subsequent scholarship (see esp. Vouaux), is now taken to be the best representative of the early *Acts of Peter*, although it cannot be simply equated with the text known to Origen and Eusebius.

HISTORY OF THE TEXT

The *Acts of Peter* was composed in Greek. Three Greek manuscripts of the *Martyrdom of Peter* have survived in hagiographic collections, where it is associated with the *Martyrdom of Paul* because the martyrdoms of the two apostles came to be celebrated on the same day. The oldest is the Patmos manuscript, Codex Patmiacus 49 (P), a menologion which dates from the ninth century. The text is given the title "Martyrdom of the Holy Apostle Peter in Rome." The narrative begins with Agrippa's plot against Peter (*Acts of Peter* 33). A second manuscript from the Vatopedi monastery on Mount Athos, Codex Athous Vatopedi 79 (A), dates from the tenth or eleventh century. It begins with the Chryse episode (*Acts of Peter* 30) and therefore includes Peter's final confrontation with Simon as well as his martyrdom. It makes brief references to some of the events narrated in earlier parts of the Vercelli *Acts*, showing that the Athos *Martyrdom* derives from a version of the *Acts of Peter* that began at ch. 4 or earlier. In the manuscript it is given the title, "Martyrdom of the Holy Apostle Peter: From the Histories of Clement, Bishop of Rome, Who Gives the History in This Manner in the Last Book." This title shows that the Martyrdom was extracted from a manuscript which combined one of the Pseudo-Clementine texts with the *Acts of Peter*, or a portion of it, in a manner similar to Vercelli manuscript. The third manuscript, Cod. Ochrid. bibl. mun. 44 (O), dates from the eleventh century and is unpublished, but apparently contains the same text type as the Patmos *Martyrdom* (Halkin, 1962: 14–16; Poupon, 1988: 4365).

In the martyrdom sections, the Greek manuscripts are to be preferred except where the Athos manuscript is clearly expansive. Additional witnesses for the *Martyrdom of Peter* are found in Syriac and Coptic, where the most complete manuscripts are similar to the Patmos *Martyrdom*, beginning with the martyrdom proper and concluding with ch. 41. Some Syriac manuscripts insert elements from the *Martyrdom of Paul*. The *Martyrdom of Peter* is also known in Armenian, Georgian, Slavonic, Russian, Arabic and Ethiopic versions (Vouaux, 1922: 15–22; Leloir, 1986). These were used to varying extents by Lipsius in his reconstruction of the text. The Latin *Passion of Peter* attributed to the bishop Linus (L) is a rather free and expansive adaptation of the *Martyrdom of Peter* based on a separate, probably later, translation from the Greek. Although it dates from the fourth century or later, it can occasionally help to establish a reading. The Pseudo-Marcellus texts, the *Acts of Peter and Paul* and the *Passion of Peter and Paul*, are further removed from the original *Acts of Peter*. For details on the manuscript evidence for all of these texts see Elliott (1993: 427–30) and Geerard (1992: 101–16).

The body of the *Acts of Peter* survives in a Latin version found in the Capitoline Museum in the north Italian town of Vercelli, Bib. cap. 108 (V). The manuscript dates from the sixth or seventh century (Baldwin, 2005: 156), but the translation probably belongs to the fourth century and may have been made in North Africa or Spain (Baldwin, 2005: 189–93; Bremmer, 1998b: 19; Poupon, 1998: 196; Thomas, 2003: 28; so already Turner, 1931: 119). Baldwin offers a detailed discussion of the language and orthography of the manuscript (174–93). In the Vercelli manuscript, the *Acts of Peter* is paired with Rufinus's translation of the Pseudo-Clementine *Recognitions*. The two documents were copied by the same scribe. The colophon of the *Recognitions* is followed by a blank page. The *Acts of Peter* begins on the next leaf, the first in a new quire, without superscription. Two leaves from the *Recognitions* are mistakenly included near the end of ch. 28. A single leaf which held most of chs. 35 and 36 is missing from the manuscript. The text is identified as the *Acts of the Apostle Peter* (*Actus Petri Apostoli*) in its explicit, although *Acts of the Apostle Peter <and Simon (et Simone)>* may have been intended. A second explicit, giving the title as the *Letter of Saint Peter with Simon Magus* (*Epistula S<an>c<t>i Petri cum Simone Mago*), is probably meant to describe the combination of the *Recognitions* and the *Acts of Peter* as a single work (Baldwin, 2005: 167–70).

The Vercelli *Acts of Peter* begins with Paul's activity in Rome and runs continuously through the martyrdom of Peter. Where it can be checked, the Latin translation generally follows the Greek word order and exhibits the usual kinds of translation and scribal errors. The quality of the late Latin has inspired, or sometimes required, scholars to offer a number of conjectural emendations throughout the text. The Latin occasionally adds phrases for clarification. It just as often deletes brief phrases. The deletions and errors are especially frequent in Peter's quasi-philosophical speeches at and on the cross. The translator apparently found these speculations uninteresting or unintelligible, perhaps both. Baldwin provides a detailed description of the manuscript and discussion of most of the parallels between the Greek and Latin texts. It is important to keep the distinctive features of the Vercelli manuscript and its translation in mind when assessing aspects of the *Acts of Peter*. However, in my judgment Baldwin's questioning of its relationship to other Petrine materials is unnecessarily restrictive.

A single vellum leaf from Oxyrhynchus (P.Oxy. 849) preserves a portion of the Greek text from a point near the end of ch. 25 through the first part of ch. 26. The manuscript dates from the late third or early fourth century (Grenfell and Hunt, 1908: 6. 6–7). Its first few lines are corrupt, but the remainder demonstrates the relative fidelity of the Latin translation and confirms the presence of one important translation error. In the Latin, the prefect states that he allowed Simon to kill the boy who was a favorite of the emperor because he had confidence in Peter and Peter's god. In the Oxyrhynchus text, the prefect's motivation is the desire to test Peter and the god who works through him.

A few additional elements outside of the martyrdom have been preserved through incorporation into later documents. The *Life of Abercius*, a fourth-century text celebrating the life of the second-century bishop of Hierapolis in Phrygia Salutaris, preserves parts of several speeches from the *Acts of Peter*. These materials are transcribed fairly directly. In the mouth of the new hero they are directed against Marcionites in the guise of Simon's disciples. Baldwin (2005: 197–241) provides the texts in parallel columns along with English translations. He offers a detailed discussion of the usefulness of the *Life* for reconstructing the Greek, or in some cases just making sense of the Latin. He notes that the Latin is often longer than the Greek, but it is impossible to know to what extent either version reflects the earlier Greek of the *Acts of Peter*.

The Syriac *History of Simon Cephas*, edited by Paul Bedjan, incorporates material from the canonical Acts, the Pseudo-Clementines and the Syriac *Teaching of Simon Cephas* as well as several episodes from the *Acts of Peter* (Bedjan, 1890: 1–44; see also Poupon, 1988: 4365). Material from chs. 8, 11, 14, 20, 22, 23, 28 and the martyrdom appears, usually in an abbreviated form. A related text (Vat. Syr. 199) incorporates additional material from the early chapters of the *Acts of Peter* (Poupon, 1988: 4366). A. de Santos Otero has called attention to number of Old Church Slavonic manuscripts of an unedited text containing material from the *Acts of Peter* (1978: 1. 52–59; see also Schneemelcher, 1992: 278; Poupon, 1988: 4367). This brief document includes material from chs. 7, 9, and 32, but the influence of the Pseudo-Marcellus *Acts of Peter and Paul* can also be seen (Lipsius, 1891: 2/1. 208–9).

The relationship of the Vercelli *Acts* to possible earlier forms of the *Acts of Peter* has received extensive discussion. The stichometry found in the *Chronography* of Nikephoros includes the *Acts of Peter* under the title *Travels of Peter* (*Periodoi Petrou*) among the New Testament apocrypha. (The stichometry lists canonical and non-canonical books, with a notation of the length of each in lines—*stichoi*.) It is unclear whether the *Chronography* should be attributed to the ninth-century Nikephoros, Archbishop of Constantinople, or to fourteenth-century Nikephoros Kallistos. Even if the later Nikephoros is the author, he was relying on a ninth-century source for the list of historical events. The *Periodoi Petrou* is assigned 2750 lines, about the length of Matthew or canonical Acts (text in Zahn, 1888: 2/1. 297–301). If this number is correct, substantial portions of the *Acts of Peter* remain unaccounted for. The missing portions are probably not as much as the one-third suggested by Theodor Zahn (843), because the Latin translation is somewhat abbreviated compared to the original Greek. On the basis of the page numbers on the Oxyrhynchus vellum leaf, Grenfell and Hunt estimated that it represented a version of the *Acts of Peter* that was about ten per cent longer than the one in the Vercelli manuscript up to that point (1908: 6. 8–9). Of course, none of these calculations is precise.

It is possible to reconstruct some of the missing content from other sources. Carl Schmidt argued that the story of Peter's daughter, preserved in the Coptic "Act of Peter" in Berlin Papyrus 8502.4, should be identified with the story mentioned by Augustine in *Contra Adimantum* 17, and that it can therefore be assigned to the *Acts of Peter* (Schmidt, 1903: 14–16). Augustine was responding to Manichaean critics of the canonical story of Ananias and Sapphira (Acts 5:1–11) by citing similar stories in books valued by his opponents:

> They condemn this with great blindness, while among the apocrypha they read as important works both the story I have mentioned about Thomas, and that the daughter of Peter himself became paralyzed through the prayers of her father, and <that> the daughter of a gardener died because of the prayer of Peter himself. They reply that this was expedient for them, that the one should be disabled by paralysis and the other die; still they do not deny that this was done through the prayers of the apostle. (text in Jolivet and Jourjon, 1961: 330)

It has been objected that Augustine does not name the source in which he found these stories (Ficker, 1904: 397; Baldwin, 2005: 96; Molinari, 2005: 82), but the context makes it likely that the *Acts of Peter* was intended (Schmidt, 1903: 14–15; Plümacher, 1978: 20–21; Poupon, 1988: 4368; Thomas, 2003: 18). Schmidt pointed to numerous parallels in theme and expression between this story and the *Acts of Peter* as it is known from the Vercelli *Acts* (Schmidt, 1903: 22–25; 1924: 321–34). He noted that the Coptic is probably closer to a translation than a paraphrase of the original Greek (1903: 21). Others have agreed with Schmidt's assessment. See the commentaries of Douglas M. Parrott, Louis Roy and Michel Tardieu. The story of Peter's daughter was probably extracted from the longer work to fill the final pages of the codex because it demonstrates the idea that God cares for his own. This theme is important throughout the *Acts of Peter*. Tardieu has shown that it is found in all four documents in the Berlin codex (1984: 19, 71).

Schmidt's proposal concerning the story of Peter's daughter has not received universal acceptance. G. Ficker questioned whether the Coptic "Act" should be assigned to the larger *Acts of Peter* (1904, 400–404). Andrea Lorenzo

Molinari has argued that the parallels adduced by Schmidt are no more than commonplaces of early Christian literature (26–59). Ironically, Molinari (32–34) succeeds in demonstrating the distinctiveness of the phrase "from her toenails to her head" used to describe the paralysis of both Peter's daughter in the Coptic "Act of Peter" (135.8–9) and of Rufina in AcPetVerc 2 (see also Thomas, 2003: 17–21). Molinari and Luttikhuizen both see significant differences between the story of Peter's daughter and the rest of the *Acts of Peter* in their attitudes toward sexuality. However, Molinari believes that the Coptic "Act" supports Christian marriage while the Vercelli *Acts* rejects it (90–91). For Luttikhuizen, it is the "uncompromising encratism" of the Coptic "Act" that stands in tension with the milder view of the rest of the *Acts of Peter* (40–41). In spite of such disagreements, the evidence has satisfied many scholars that this story indeed belonged to the original *Acts of Peter* (Poupon, 1988: 4368; Thomas, 2003: 18–20).

Domitien de Bruyne (1908: 153) argued that the story of a gardener and his daughter, also mentioned by Augustine, is reflected in the Pseudo-Titus epistle on virginity and in an aphorism attributed to Peter in the thirteenth-century florilegium, Codex Cambray 254. The Pseudo-Titus epistle treats its borrowed narratives, including a probable reference to the story of Rufina familiar from AcPetVerc 2, in a very free and summary fashion. The quotation in Codex Cambray employs language that is not found elsewhere in the *Acts of Peter*; it probably gives only a very indirect reflection of the original. These summaries can only suggest the content of the original story. They cannot be used to reconstruct the wording of the text. Two other Petrine sayings published later by De Bruyne (1933) are probably not related to the *Acts of Peter* in any way.

In light of the mention of Peter's twelve-year stay in Jerusalem (AcPetVerc 5), Schmidt argued that the original *Acts of Peter* was organized into two parts, set in Jerusalem and Rome respectively. He believed that the Jerusalem section was dropped from the Vercelli version in order to make a smoother transition from the Pseudo-Clementine *Recognitions*, which precede it in the manuscript. This truncation would explain why the Latin version is so much shorter than the length assigned by Nikephoros. Schmidt assigned the stories of Peter's daughter and the gardener's daughter to this Jerusalem portfolio, in part because of the reference to Peter's house in the first of those stories. Schmidt further argued that the story of Eubula, narrated in Peter's speech in ch. 17, recounts events narrated at greater length earlier in the Jerusalem section. In the Latin version, the story is set in Judea, but Schmidt saw the reference to the Neapolis gate as evidence for the more specific identification of the city (1926: 499–501). The Eubula episode is explicitly located in Jerusalem in the Syriac *History of Simon Cephas* (Bedjan, 1890: 18, 20). Schmidt found additional evidence for the content of the missing section in ch. 23, arguing that the reference to a meeting between Peter and Simon in Jerusalem suggested that an account of the event had been given earlier. He found this story to be reflected in the Syriac *Didascalia* 6.7–9 also (Schmidt, 1903: 146–48; 1926: 507). Because this is the only reference to Peter and Paul acting together in the surviving portions of the *Acts of Peter*, Vouaux (1922: 32) questioned its originality.

Disagreements continue concerning how much material dealing with Peter's activity in Jerusalem remains unaccounted for and where one might hope to find it. While some have sought evidence of the missing material in the Pseudo-Clementine literature or, for example, in the *Acts of Peter and the Twelve Apostles* (so Krause, 1972), no convincing example has been brought forward. Other documents reporting the activities of Peter, such as the Slavic *Life of Peter* (Franko, 1902: 316–24), the Syriac "Voyages" (Nau, 1909: 131–34) or *Acts of Peter and Andrew*, seem to have little or no relationship to the *Acts of Peter* known from the Vercelli *Acts* (Poupon, 1988: 4364).

In 2006, François Bovon and Bertrand Bouvier published the first critical edition of brief Greek text from a manuscript in the Angelica Library in Rome, *Angelicus graecus* 108. They asked whether it might derive from the *Acts of Peter*. The document bears the title "From the Acts of the Holy Apostle Peter," but as Bovon and Bouvier note, there is a rich field of Petrine texts that are independent of the *Acts* attested in the Vercelli manuscript (23). In the Angelicus *Act*, Peter is traveling to Azot when he encounters the prince of demons and seven of his subordinates, all of whom are disguised as angels. When questioned, Satan identifies himself as the archangel of justice and names the virtues supposedly represented by four of the others. Peter, however, recognizes Satan. By means of prayer, the sign of the cross, and a circle drawn around them, he constrains the demons and compels them to reveal their true identities as the spirits responsible for major sins. After a week of imprisonment, during which there is no sin on earth, the demons are released to continue testing the faith of Christians (ch. 11). The text concludes with a brief homily that is probably a secondary expansion.

There are parallels between the Angelica *Act* and the Vercelli *Acts* in that Peter's failures of faith are pointed out (ch. 2), and Satan identifies himself by reciting a long list of his deceptions drawn from the Old and New Testaments (ch. 4). Bovon and Bouvier acknowledge that the list of major sins is hard to date (28–31) and that the manner in which Peter signs the cross probably reflects later practice (34–36). But both details are things that could have been modified in the process of transmission. It is not clear, however, how a journey to Azot would fit into the scheme of the early *Acts of Peter*, which apparently depicted Peter as remaining in Jerusalem for twelve years prior to his journey to Rome. More importantly, the exchange between Peter and Satan is conceived differently in in this new text. While Peter is able to defeat "the whole power of Simon and his god" (AcPetVerc 22), the confrontation is less direct and the victory is only local. The notion that Christ gives demons free range to test the faithful seems contrary to the emphasis placed the care shown by God and Christ in the Vercelli *Acts*. Bovon and Bouvier note that the closest parallels to the Angelica *Act* are found in the *History of Peter and Paul*, which is preserved in Arabic and other oriental versions (25–28). A translation of the Arabic version was published by Lewis (1904: 175–92). In the *History*, Satan assumes the form of an Indian prince accompanied by an entourage of disguised demons. It is unlikely that either of these narratives derives from the *Acts of Peter* as represented in the Vercelli *Acts*.

The more difficult question is whether substantial material may have been added to an earlier form of the *Acts of Peter* before the translation into Latin was made. The question asked most frequently is whether the first three chapters and the final chapter belonged to the original text or should be considered secondary additions. Harnack (1900: 100–106) first proposed this as a way of dealing with Jesus' saying, "I am about to be crucified again," which is attributed to the *Acts of Paul* in Origen. Harnack argued that the closely parallel saying in AcPetVerc 35, was derived from the *Acts of Paul*. He interpreted the appearances of Paul in AcPetVerc 1–3 and 41 as evidence of such borrowing. Ficker rejected both Harnack's suggestion and Schmidt's Jerusalem hypothesis because he judged that the first three chapters represent the original opening and were intended to link the *Acts of Peter* to the canonical Acts (Ficker, 1903: 7; 1904: 397; see also Michaelis, 1964: 317, 321–22). Schmidt defended his view (Schmidt, 1926: 494–513). Meanwhile, Vouaux took a middle position. He accepted the authenticity of the story of Peter's daughter and a Jerusalem section (1922: 35–41). He refined Schmidt's hypothesis with the suggestion that when the *Acts of Peter* was shortened the story of Eubula was transposed from its original context to Peter's speech in AcPetVerc 17, where it replaced a brief allusion to the event (1922: 33–35). Schmidt responded that the full speech is necessary in the present context and that a more complete version of the story probably stood in the Jerusalem section (1926: 503–4). On the other hand, Vouaux believed the first three chapters had been added to the abbreviated form in order to tie it to the conclusion of the canonical Acts (1922: 27–33). He also suspected the originality of the AcPetVerc 41. Vouaux noted that if chs. 1–3 and 41 are not original, the remaining references to Paul could be easily removed (1922: 28).

Schmidt's discovery of a version of the *Quo vadis* scene that has Jesus saying, "I am about to be crucified again," among the portions of the *Acts of Paul* preserved in the Hamburg papyrus removed Harnack's grounds for suspecting the originality of chs. 1–3 and 41 (1930: 151). Schmidt argued that the version in the *Acts of Peter* should be seen as the source of the motif in the *Acts of Paul*. He modified his dating of the *Acts of Peter* in light of this new understanding of the relationship between the texts, arguing now for a date between 180 and 192 c.e. (1930: 154). Poupon has adopted and refined Vouaux's analysis, supporting the argument with evidence of editorial activity in the relevant passages (1988: 4370–82). Poupon agrees with Vouaux that Peter's speech in ch. 17 has been transposed from its original place in the Jerusalem section, and suggests that the brief reference in the Syriac *History of Simon Cephas* might reflect the original wording of ch. 17 (1988: 4365 n. 14). Poupon also agreed with Vouaux that the reference to Paul in AcPetVerc 23 is secondary. He suggested that the original wording of this scene is also reflected in the Syriac *History of Simon Cephas* (1988: 4372), where Simon is said to have been confronted by Peter and the other apostles in Jerusalem. Because the other apostles are not named, it is not likely that Paul is meant. Poupon further notes the confusion about the status of Marcellus as a believer in ch. 10, and suggests that the story has been modified to make Marcellus a lapsed believer (1988: 4375–76). It should be noted, however, that Ptolemy's status as a believer in the story of Peter's daughter is equally ambiguous. Christine M. Thomas follows most of Poupon's arguments, but she shows that the changes would have been made in the Greek text before the translation into Latin (2003: 21–27). Poupon's suggestion that the story of Chryse is secondary because it disrupts the chronological sequence of the narrative (1988: 4377–78) has not found acceptance.

The final chapter (AcPetMart 12 = AcPetVerc 41) is suspect in the eyes of many because of the role played by members of Caesar's household and because Peter's death is associated with Nero. Interest in the imperial household suggests borrowing from the *Acts of Paul*, but the motif is present in the AcPetVerc 3, where it is also connected with Paul and, more importantly, in the AcPetVerc 26, where the young man killed by Simon is identified as a favorite of Caesar's. Indeed, the use of this motif in the *Acts of Peter* is closer to (canonical) Phil 1:13 than to the explicitly military language of the *Martyrdom of Paul*.

As for chronology, the tension among AcPetVerc 1, 5 and 41 is perhaps more acute for modern readers than it would have been for the ancient author or audience. If the twelve years mentioned in Peter's vision in the AcPetVerc 5 are counted from death of Jesus, Peter should arrive in Rome under Claudius. Because the *Acts of Peter* gives the impression of that Peter's stay in Rome was brief, his martyrdom under Nero seems inconsistent. However, in AcPetVerc 1 the voice from heaven does not limit Paul's time in Spain to a single year. It is not clear whether that aspect of the believers' prayer is answered or not. The voice simply indicates the Paul will work there for the rest of his life. Nero is identified as an evil man, but not as the emperor at the time of Paul's departure. The *Acts of Peter* is simply not explicit about the amount of time separating the death of Simon from the martyrdom of Peter. The summary of miracles at the beginning of the AcPetVerc 31 could cover almost any length of time. Later tradition, which placed Peter in Rome for twenty-five years, did not reject the *Acts of Peter*. Both the *Teaching of Simon Cephas in the City of Rome* and the *History of Simon Cephas* simply add a few lines after the miracle summary noting that Peter built the churches of Rome and Italy to fill the apparent gap. AcPetVerc 41 is present in all three Greek manuscripts and is evidenced in most versions in other languages. So the arguments against the originality are not conclusive, and something like Nero's vision is necessary to provide a positive ending. The death of an important figure was expected to bring an end to persecution (cf. *Mart. Pol.* 1:1).

The originality of the first three chapters has been questioned because they deal with Paul rather than Peter. But there is no *a priori* reason why apostolic acts should deal with a single apostle, as both canonical Acts and the later *Acts of Philip* demonstrate. The material which has Paul as its hero shows the same range of concerns as the rest of the *Acts of Peter*. If the original beginning of the work has been lost, Paul's appearance in the opening chapters is less surprising. Poupon has argued that concern for the issue of returning apostates (*lapsi*) motivated expansion of the work, and the addition of Paul in particular (1988 4378–82; cf. Thomas, 2003: 23–27). Without the first three chapters the theme of returning lapsed Christians to the faith would be weakened, but it would not eliminated. It is important in every part of the narrative (Perkins, 1995; 1997; already Schmidt 1903: 162).

As for the relation between the *Acts of* Peter and canonical Acts, although AcPetVerc 1–3 can be read as building on the end of Acts it is unlikely that the *Acts of Peter* was conceived as a continuation of it. The transposition of Peter's encounter with Simon from Samaria to Jerusalem (AcPetVerc 23) suggests that the Lukan Acts was not a definitive authority to the author. Schmidt's suggestion that the choice to begin with Paul's departure from Rome was made when the *Acts of Peter* was truncated—to follow more logically from the Pseudo-Clementine *Recognitions*—is a simpler explanation of the state of the text (Schmidt, 1926: 509–12).

The Vercelli *Acts*, including chs. 1–3 and 41, together with the Coptic "Act of Peter" and the story of the gardener's daughter, should be taken as the best evidence for the original *Acts of Peter* available. Together they probably represent most of the original content of the *Acts of Peter*. Nevertheless, because there are so few manuscripts, it is easy to get the impression that we have something closer to the original than is actually the case. Studies of the *Acts of Peter* need to take into account the uncertainties concerning the text's history. Every manuscript we have presents a version that has been transformed in the course of truncation, expansion, and/or, translation. Thomas prefers to treat each witness as a separate performance and emphasizes the fluidity of the narrative (2003: 40–71). Baldwin argues that the Vercelli manuscript should be interpreted in its own terms as a distinctive "instantiation" of the Petrine tradition (2005: 60–62, 302–3). These approaches are important for understanding how the various versions of the *Acts of Peter* were employed. They urge caution, but they do not preclude the possibility of reconstructing the text within reasonable limits.

CONTENTS AND STRUCTURE

The structure of the surviving portions of the *Acts of Peter* is clear in spite of the questions about the extent of the original. The various stories and speeches are organized around the competition between the apostle Peter and Simon Magus, which is followed by the martyrdom of the apostle. The contest embodies the central message of the work by showing that Christ offers benefits to his followers that are superior to those available from either Simon or Roman society. Many of the miracle stories employ older traditions, but they are all interpreted as signs of Christ's care for the faithful in both material and spiritual matters. Most of the vision reports are the author's creations, designed to document the availability and importance of divine guidance. Both types of story are also used to show the possibility of forgiveness and a return to faith, even after apostasy (see Stoops, 1986; 1991. The author clearly enjoys interweaving stories, sometimes at the expense of a clear plotline.

Significant blocks of speech material appear alongside the narratives, but neither Peter nor Simon expounds a coherent theological position. Simon's speeches are more denunciations of Christianity than positive presentations of an alternative. Peter's speeches range from retelling miracles and visions to preaching and apologetics. Peter's prayers and exorcisms may reflect liturgical usage in the author's community, but it is impossible to locate them precisely. Peter's speeches at and from the cross make greater use imagery borrowed from middle-Platonism, which suggests that some special exegetical traditions, or even written sources, lie behind these discourses. When secondary characters such as Marcellus or Ariston are given short speeches, they merely interpret events in the immediate context.

Earlier versions of the *Acts of Peter* probably opened with a substantial block of material set in Jerusalem, especially in light of the note that Peter had been ordered to stay in the city for twelve years (AcPetVerc 5). Efforts to reconstruct a Jerusalem section remain speculative. If it contained a commissioning scene, it was not comparable to those of the later acts (Junod, 1981a: 234, 238, 242; Kaestli, 1981b: 262). An account of Peter's daughter similar to, if not largely identical with, the "Act of Peter" in P.Berol. 8502,4 can reasonably be assigned to Jerusalem even though the *Acts of Saints Nereus and Achilleus* locates its greatly expanded version of the story of Peter's daughter in Rome. While the first part of the story in P.Berol. 8502,4 is built around a chastity story, the surrounding stories introduce additional themes that are important throughout the *Acts of Peter*. Both the daughter's paralysis and Ptolemy's healing are presented as proof of God's providence. Miracles performed on the physical level are interpreted as signs of the greater spiritual benefits available from the same source and serve to strengthen the faith of the crowd. The possibility of forgiveness, even after serious offenses, is emphasized in the story of Ptolemy. Finally, the story demonstrates the proper use of material riches for the benefit of the community of believers. The whole episode is interpreted by Peter himself as proof that God takes care of the faithful, even when that care is not immediately apparent, an idea that is found throughout the *Acts of Peter*.

A version of the story of the gardener's daughter probably belonged to the Jerusalem section as well. It apparently related purity to providence in much the same way as did the story of Peter's daughter. Neither of these stories involves Simon Magus, but remarks made later, in AcPetVerc 5 and 23, suggests that the Jerusalem section also included scenes in which Simon was confronted by Peter, possibly in the company of Paul or other apostles (see above). The Jerusalem material probably reached its climax with Eubula's conversion and Simon's flight from Judea. Much of the narrative in ch. 17 may have originally belonged to this section. The story is referred to in ch. 5 as though it were already familiar. Eubula's experiences provide proof that Simon is a greedy charlatan. Her story also shows that prominent people can recognize Peter's God and turn their wealth to the service of the poor. It therefore appears that the major interests of the *Acts of Peter* were well established before the action moved to Rome.

The first three chapters of the Vercelli *Acts* narrate Paul's activity in Rome and his departure for Spain. In the Vercelli manuscript these chapters serve as an awkward transition from the Pseudo-Clementine *Recognitions*, which ends with Simon fleeing from Peter in Antioch. A voice from heaven predicts Paul's death at hands of Nero, but rather surprisingly does not suggest a close link between the martyrdoms of the two apostles. The story of Rufina in ch. 2 supplies another chastity story. Like the story of Peter's daughter in the Berlin codex, it leads to Paul's pronouncement of the possibility of repentance and forgiveness even after grave sin. Paul's speech serves to strengthen the faith of the recently converted. As Paul departs, in a scene that foreshadows the subplot around Marcellus, the senator Demetrios laments the fact that his office prevents him from following the apostle. Paul's journey to Spain sets the stage for Simon's corruption of the Christians of Rome. By placing Paul in Rome ahead of Peter, the author shows that even believers who had benefitted from apostolic instruction were vulnerable to Simon's deceit. More importantly, the narrative can assure the audience that a return to faith is possible after apostasy as well as other sin.

Nothing, then, suggests that the missing portions of the *Acts of Peter* contained more extensive narratives of Paul's activities, whether in Jerusalem or in Rome. The mention of Paul's conflicts with Jewish teachers and his imprisonment are probably drawn from the Lukan Acts. In the Pseudo-Marcellus texts, conflicts with the Jews provide the motivation for the martyrdoms of both apostles, but no specific confrontations which might reflect missing portions of the *Acts of Peter* are narrated.

Within days of Paul's departure, Simon's spectacular entrance into the city raises questions about his identity (AcPetVerc 4). Most of the Roman faithful fall away, believing Simon to be either a divine being or the messenger of the true god. A similar confusion concerning Peter's status will appear in AcPetVerc 5:14 and 29:1. Peter correctly identifies Simon as the messenger of Satan (AcPetVerc 3:21; see also 17:56; 18:3). Peter, of course, is the authentic messenger of God, having been directed by Christ to travel to Rome and confront Simon (ch. 5). The conversion of the ship's captain en route offers a model response to the apostle's teaching. Peter is met at the harbor by Ariston, who reports that Simon has corrupted most of the Christians in the city along with many others (ch. 6). Ariston also reports a vision that has assured him that Christ will rebuild the community of believers through Peter.

The contest in Rome (AcPetVerc 7–32) begins with Peter's address to those who had been seduced by Simon. The speech provides a summary of the author's interests. Peter employs a veritable grab-bag of apologetic arguments to convert, and reconvert, the Romans. Appeals to the Hebrew prophets and the virgin birth stand beside language that equates redemption with dispelling ignorance. Listeners are warned of the devil's power to deceive and are reminded of their need to repent. To drive his point home, Peter cites himself as the leading example of one whose faith, though once inadequate, has now been strengthened. Peter contends that deeds provide more certain ground for faith than words, thereby justifying the predominance of miracles throughout the *Acts of Peter*. The enthusiastic reaction of the crowd doubtless indicates the response the author hoped to evoke from those who read or heard these stories.

Before the major public battles between Peter and Simon Magus begin, several minor skirmishes take place. These events make room for the subplot centered on the senator Marcellus (AcPetVerc 8–14). Through a series of interwoven stories, Marcellus is made the leading example of a human patron who deserves gratitude but is unable to provide spiritual leadership. His material wealth and high social status repeatedly interfere with his loyalty to Christ. Marcellus has risked losing the favor of his imperial patron through his material support of the believers. However, the conflict of loyalties he experiences is not presented in the absolute terms of conflicting kingdoms found, for example, in the *Martyrdom of Paul*. Marcellus speaks of having paid for instruction, but it is not clear that he is thought to have become a Christian himself (AcPetVerc 10).

By the time Peter arrives in Rome, Marcellus, has abandoned the believers and become Simon's patron. His change of mind is blamed for leading many of the believers into the same error. Upon arrival at Marcellus's house, Peter employs a speaking dog to expose Simon, who is hiding inside. Marcellus pleads for forgiveness, appealing to Peter's own famous doubts as a precedent for repentance. Here he seems to speak as though he had earlier been a believer. Peter prays for Marcellus and embraces him. The scene is interrupted when one of the bystanders laughs (ch. 11). Peter recognizes the presence of a demon, and proceeds with an exorcism. When the departing spirit destroys a statue of the emperor, Marcellus reveals the weakness of his faith by expressing fear of reprisals. Peter guides Marcellus as he successfully restores the statue through prayer and lustration. In AcPetVerc12 the story reverts to the dog, who is still in the house denouncing Simon and predicting his ultimate destruction. The dog then returns to Peter outside the house, where he dies after predicting both Peter's victory over Simon and the apostle's martyrdom.

Peter has no chance to react to this news, because the crowd demands another sign. Peter responds by bringing a dried fish to life. In consequence of this, many in the crowd convert and receive instruction from Peter in the house of the presbyter Narcissus (AcPetVerc 13). It is only after Marcellus's faith has been confirmed by additional signs the he finally expels Simon from his house and purifies the building for use by the community. Although Marcellus once again turns his wealth to the support of believers, he never reaches a point where he can be trusted in matters of faith.

Soon, Simon seeks out Peter at the house of the presbyter Narcissus. He is met by a mother and her newborn child. The infant, like the dog, speaks with a prophetic voice to condemn Simon and predict the public contest. In a final irony, the ordinarily speechless child speaks in the name of Jesus to deprive Simon of speech and expel him from Rome (AcPetVerc 15).

Simon's expulsion from the city by the power of God provides an interlude for Peter's further ministry of teaching and healing (AcPetVerc 16–22). Peter receives divine assurance that miracles will be given through him for the conversion of many. When he recounts this vision to the faithful, Peter adds a review of Simon's attempt to defraud the rich widow Eubula and his subsequent flight from Judea when his deceptions were exposed (ch. 17). The reminder of Christ's constant presence introduces the description of a worship service in the house of Marcellus, which becomes the occasion both for the healing of blind widows and for Peter's exegesis of the transfiguration story (chs. 20–21).

Both of these stories demonstrate the link between physical and spiritual healing through illumination. Christ's polymorphism—that is his appearance in different forms to different people, even at the same time—is an important feature in many of the early apocryphal acts (Cartlidge, 1986). In the *Acts of Peter* the motif is used to confirm Christ's accessibility to and care for all. In stark contrast, Marcellus has a dream which reveals how concern for his senatorial rank still makes it difficult for him to do God's will.

The dramatic contest in the forum (AcPetVerc 23–28) offers another condensed version of the whole work. Members of every social order attend, paying a gold coin apiece to see the show. Peter reminds Simon of their past encounters. Simon repeats his denunciation of Jesus as nothing more than an obscure carpenter who suffered crucifixion. Peter responds by saying that it is necessary to understand the prophets. The debate quickly collapses into a contest of miracles. The fickle crowd has to be taught to distinguish the truly miraculous operation of divine power from the merely magical manipulations of a charlatan. In chs. 25–26 the prefect, later identified as Agrippa, puts forward a young man, who becomes speechless and dies when Simon whispers in his ear. Just when Peter is ready to raise the boy, a Christian widow bursts upon the scene lamenting that her only son has died. Peter sends a group of men to fetch the body, and then directs the prefect to raise Simon's victim. The crowd responds with praise for "the one God of Peter." The widow's son is raised in ch. 27. Before the crowd has a chance to disperse, a second widow appears. Her son, a young senator, has also died. Again the body is brought to the forum. This time Peter challenges Simon to raise the dead. Simon is able to make the corpse move, which turns the crowd against Peter. They are ready to burn him. Peter chastises the crowd for their credulity and shows that the boy is not truly alive. After securing the mother's promise that the slaves freed for the young man's funeral will retain their freedom, Peter raises her son. Both mother and son make substantial donations to support the Christian women residing in Marcellus's house (ch. 29).

The multiplication of resurrections demonstrates Christ's accessibility to people at all levels of society, from slaves and poor widows to wealthy senatorial families (Stoops, 1986; see also Thomas, 1998). The wealthy are reminded of their obligation to respond to Christ's benefactions by caring for the widows and virgins. The story of Chryse (AcPetVerc 30) shows plainly that concern for the issues of benefaction and patronage overrides interest in purity in the *Acts of Peter*. Chryse's gift is accepted as a spiritual debt owed to Christ in spite of her notorious sexual license.

A summary of Peter's miracles leads to a second, climactic confrontation with Simon. Simon too performs wonders and ultimately promises to show his true nature by ascending to heaven. The use of the title "Standing One" in this episode suggests that the author had some information, albeit possibly indirect, about Simon's actual teachings. When a crowd gathers on the *via sacra*, Simon repeats his denunciation of Christ as weak and unworthy, and then rises into the air. When Peter intervenes with a prayer, the sorcerer comes crashing down to earth. Finally defeated, Simon departs from Rome and, shortly thereafter, from life.

The narrative of Peter's martyrdom, beginning in ch. 33 of the Vercelli *Acts*, introduces a different set of emphases. Peter's message of purity includes abstinence from sex, or at least from inappropriate sexual relations. Among those who accept Peter's preaching on purity are four concubines of the prefect Agrippa, a figure who had earlier seemed favorably disposed or neutral toward Peter (chs. 26, 28). When Agrippa's friend Albinus complains that his wife has also withdrawn from his bed as a result of Peter's preaching, the two Romans conspire against the apostle. The events motivating the plot for Peter's death are not necessarily an endorsement of an encratite ethic. It is clear that concubinage would be deemed impure by most Christians. Because Albinus is explicitly described as driven mad by lust, the episode need not be seen as a condemnation of marriage or even of normal sexual relations within marriage. (Compare Justin's account of the martyrdom of the Christian teacher Ptolemy in *2 Apology* 2.)

An alternative explanation is that Peter is accused of being an atheist and a meddler. Specifically, Peter's teaching has led to a violation of the male householder's authority (Czachesz in Bremmer, 1998a: 91).The prefect of the city, if that is what Agrippa is imagined to be, would have the authority to execute a provincial on the second charge. The whole section is meant to demonstrate the base motives of those responsible for Peter's martyrdom, although, of course, it is also shown to be God's will. When the plot against the apostle is discovered, Peter is convinced to withdraw from Rome (cf. *Mart. Pol.* 5:1). He is met at the city gate by Christ in the famous *Quo vadis* scene. When Christ says that he is coming to Rome to be crucified again, Peter understands and willingly returns to face arrest and execution (cf. *Mart. Pol.* 5:2).

Curiously, many of the elements most commonly found in martyrdom accounts are missing from the *Martyrdom of Peter*. There is no trial, nor any confession of "the name (*sc.* of Christ)". Rather, the speeches which make up the bulk of the *Martyrdom* are introduced as revelations of mysteries previously kept hidden within Peter's soul (AcPetMart 8[37]–10[39]). The christological titles addressed to the cross are followed by an explanation of Peter's inverted execution as an emblem of birth into the realm of becoming (see J. Z. Smith, 1970). These speeches interpret the history of salvation in terms drawn from middle-Platonism. It is not necessary to read them as gnostic speculation, especially since they do not match any known gnostic system. Peter concludes his speech and his life with a thanksgiving and a final exhortation to look to Christ for the ultimate spiritual gifts. When Marcellus prepares Peter's body and places it in his own tomb, Peter appears to him at night to rebuke him. In this manner, Marcellus and his money are put in their place for the last time. In the final chapter, Nero begins to persecute the believers in his anger over the conversion of some of his slaves. The persecution is ended when Nero has a vision of a figure scourging him in the night. The episode thus serves to document the peace brought to the church by the apostle's death (cf. *Mart. Pol.* 1:1).

It is unlikely that either Paul's return to Rome or martyrdom was narrated in the original *Acts of Peter*, although both are predicted within the text. AcPetMart 12(41) is present in all of the versions of the *Martyrdom of Peter*, but there is no manuscript evidence that the *Martyrdom of Peter* continued beyond this point apart from some Syriac manuscripts that insert a section taken from the *Martyrdom of Paul*. Later texts that reflect the linkage of the deaths of Peter and Paul in the liturgical calendar borrow from both the *Martyrdom of Peter* and the *Martyrdom of Paul*.

LITERARY CHARACTER

The debate over the best approach to understanding the apocryphal acts has run parallel to the discussions of the New Testament gospels and Acts. Some scholars principally pursue the question of *genre*, asking which literary models informed the authors of the apocryphal acts (Bovon, 1981b, 141; 1988: 26). Others see these texts as more loosely structured collections of traditions, thus best studied with the methods of form criticism (Schneemelcher, 1992b: 78 –83) or folklore (MacDonald, 1983; Burrus, 1987).

Whether the *Acts of Peter* can be assigned to a recognized genre of literature remains an open question, in spite of extensive discussion. Ernst von Dobschütz (1902) first suggested that the early apocryphal acts belong to the genre of romance or novel. However, the story types and themes that von Dobschütz and others (Söder, Blumenthal, Plümacher) associated with romance are not as prominent in the *Acts of Peter* as in the other early apocryphal acts. The erotic motif, even in ascetic guise, appears in only a few stories. Chastity is more taken for granted than argued. No exotic lands are visited, and the single journey takes place without mishap. Apart from Peter's own martyrdom, only Paul is imprisoned, and no one is enslaved. While miracles and talking beasts do play an important role in the *Acts of Peter*, these elements are not unique to romance and cannot by themselves define the larger genre.

Because Hellenistic and Roman novels incorporate many different literary and non-literary forms (Hock in Aune, 1988: 133–34), more recent attempts to define the genre have focused on narrative structure and function. B. E. Perry (1967: 18) and B. P. Reardon (1991: 169–75) interpret the pattern of separation and return as a means of addressing the isolation of the individual in a complex world. Be that as it may, the author of the *Acts of Peter* either did not recognize, or did not choose to exploit, the journey as a device for tying together separate stories. The possibilities for combining a contest with a journey were more fully worked out in the Pseudo-Clementine literature. Ronald F. Hock (in Aune, 1988: 134) focuses on the humiliation and subsequent exaltation of the protagonists. Because Peter is consistently victorious in his encounters with Simon, the contest structure in the *Acts of Peter* appears to be designed for the promotion of Christianity rather than the psychological integration of an individual into society. The novelistic elements in the apocryphal acts may function to support the individual's separation from the larger society in order to establish a closer tie to the transcendent realm (Perkins, 1997). While the *Acts of Peter* depicts a community of believers that is both loyal to and dependent on God and Christ, it is not hostile to the larger world (Stoops, 1986; 1991).

Ancient lives of philosophers have also been investigated as a possible model for the apocryphal acts, beginning with Reitzenstein (1963). The parallels are not as precise as might be wished in this case either (see Junod, 1981b). It seems more productive to look at the larger genre of biography. A "life" often narrated the great deeds and teachings of the founder or representative of a group and might include many different types of material (Aune, 1988: 110, 123–24). Biographical works which might be considered comparable to the *Acts of Peter* include Philostratus's *Life of Apollonius* and the New Testament gospels (Bovon, 1981; so already Koester, 1971: 190–92). The most instructive examples may be Lucian's *Alexander the False Prophet* and *Life of Peregrinus*, both of which use biographical sketches as a form of negative religious propaganda. In sum, the *Acts of Peter* can be considered biographical to the extent that it focuses on a portion of Peter's career and his death, but it is not a classic "life story" (see further Aune, 1988: 123–25).

Other scholars have inquired whether the authors of the apocryphal acts were significantly motivated by any desire to imitate established literary models (Kaestli, 1981a). Wilhelm Schneemelcher, in particular, has stressed the non-literary, or popular, character of these texts. He argues that they are best understood as collections of independent traditions and has called for form-critical studies. Schneemelcher holds that representatives of local churches were responsible for the transmission of the underlying traditions (1992b: 83). Others have suggested that opponents of those local authorities, especially women, stand behind the present texts (Davies, 1980; MacDonald, 1983; Burrus, 1987). Any attempt to identify traditions belonging to local churches is of course complicated by the tendency within the tradition to add, or change, specific locales for such things as the place of Peter's martyrdom (as in the later *Passion of Peter*) or of his daughter's burial (*Acts of Nereus and Achilleus* 15). The *Acts of Peter* appears to incorporate a variety of materials which circulated in different contexts. The range of traditions employed makes it unlikely that a single community can be identified behind this text. It cannot even be assumed that all of the elements had specific connections to Peter prior to their use in the present text, since several of the stories were also attached to other figures in roughly contemporary texts. So, for example, the exorcism in AcPetVerc 11 has a close parallel in Philostratus's *Life of Apollonius* 4.20. A variant of the fish story in the AcPetVerc 13 is told of Jesus in the Latin *Infancy Gospel of Thomas*. Molinari has identified partial parallels to the story of Peter's daughter in Roman literature (2005: 124–56).

It seems clear, first, that the traditional materials that can be identified in the miracle stories and speeches reflect many different interests, and second, that they show signs of having been modified to serve the needs of the author (Stoops, 1986; 1991). Some of the prayers and ritual formulas may reflect practices in the author's community. However, liturgical elements, such as the various titles used of Christ and God, are easily changed to match the interests of scribes and translators. In light of this, it is particularly interesting that L. H. Westra (in Bremmer, 1998a) has found that the creedal formulae in the *Acts of Peter* have their closest parallels in the second century.

The growing recognition that literary genres, including romance and biography, were both fluid and eclectic in the second and third centuries c.e. reduces the urgency of the genre question for the apocryphal acts (Junod and Kaestli, 1983: 683). There was a good deal of cross-fertilization between oral tradition and written texts in early Christianity. As material passed back and forth between oral and written media it was subject to roughly the same rules in each context (Koester, 1977: 286–87). Stories and ideas moved between the two media for centuries, but the exchange seems to have been particularly heavy in the period during which the apocryphal acts were written. The process did not stop with the composition of the text we are calling the *Acts of Peter* (Thomas, 2003: 40–71). In light of these facts, the *Acts of Peter* should not be treated as a mere collection of anecdotes. But neither should it be seen as a failed attempt to create a great piece of literature. The *Acts of Peter* was not out of place in its larger literary environment. Indeed, G. W. Bowersock (1994) has suggested that the apocryphal acts of apostles may have influenced the development of the Greek novels rather than the other way around.

AUTHOR, DATE
AND PROVENANCE

The identity of the author, or authors, of the *Acts of Peter* remains a mystery. Photios's attribution of the five major apocryphal acts to Leucius Charinos is not plausible due to the differences among them (Junod, 1981a). Even the less ambitious claim that Leucius produced both the *Acts of John* and the *Acts of Peter* overlooks important differences in style and content. Some manuscripts connect the *Acts of Peter* with Clement of Rome, but only because it is treated as a continuation of the Pseudo-Clementine "Histories." We have no indications of the author's, or authors', status or personality beyond the obvious ability to compose such a work. He or she shows some familiarity with popular literary forms but was not necessarily highly educated. Efforts to locate the sources and authors of apocryphal acts among communities of Christian women (Davies, 1980; MacDonald, 1983; Burrus, 1987) are not fully persuasive and are probably less relevant to the *Acts of Peter* than to the *Acts of Paul*. They do show that we cannot presume to know even the gender of the author. The concerns expressed in the text are those of the broad church rather than any identifiable sect.

It may be argued that the use of testimony lists of Old Testament prophecies and gospel literature indicates that he or she was more deeply steeped in "orthodox" Christian traditions than the authors of the *Acts of John* or the *Acts of Andrew*. However, these differences may simply reflect a different approach to apologetics. The lack of interest in Jewish customs and the treatment of

Jews as outsiders suggest that the author was a Gentile writing for a largely Gentile church. Paul is said to have overcome the Jewish teachers in the Ac-PetVerc 1. The author is aware that Jesus and his apostles were Jews, but calls Simon a Jew as well (ch. 6). It is worthy of note that the public contests take place on the Sabbath, and before a mixed crowd of Jews and Gentiles, but gatherings for worship take place on the first day of the week. i.e., on Sunday, the Lord's day (P.Berol. 8502, 128; AcPetVerc 7:1).

EXTERNAL EVIDENCE FOR
THE DATE OF COMPOSITION

The evidence for the use of the *Acts of Peter* prior to Eusebius's citation of Origen (*Hist. eccl.* 3.1.2) is far from secure. Traditions similar to those in the *Acts of Peter* are found in Clement of Alexandria and Hippolytus at the beginning of the third century, but dependence on the *Acts of Peter* cannot be demonstrated in either case. Clement mentions Peter's daughter (*Strom.* 3.6.52). He also reports that Peter encouraged his wife toward martyrdom (*Strom.* 7.11.63), an event not found in the *Acts of Peter* as we have it. Elsewhere, Clement cites a text called the *Preaching of Peter* (*Keryma Petrou*) and probably had additional sources of Petrine tradition to draw on. Hippolytus, writing in Rome around the year 200 c.e., offers both a closer parallel and a clearer contrast. After describing Simon's teachings and methods of allegorical interpretation, Hippolytus gives a brief summary of Simon's activity in Rome including his opposition by Peter (*Haer.* 6). However, his account of Simon's death is significantly different from that in the *Acts of Peter*. It more clearly presents Simon as an antichrist. Simon is buried alive by his disciples, promising to return after three days, which, of course, he fails to do. While Hippolytus may have drawn on the *Acts of Peter* (Schmidt, 1903: 104), it is probable that he worked with an independent tradition (Schneemelcher, 1992a: 272). It may be added that Hippolytus complained about apocrypha being written in his own time (Eusebius *Hist. eccl.* 4.22.9), although it is impossible to know which texts he had in mind.

The Muratorian canon list is often associated with Rome and dated as early as 200 c.e., in which case it could support the claim that Hippolytus knew the *Acts of Peter*. Unfortunately, neither the location nor the date of composition of this fragment is certain. The list does not mention the *Acts of Peter* by name but states the following:

> But the acts of all the apostles are written in one book. (Writing) for the most excellent Theophilus, Luke summarizes the various things that happened in his own presence, as he makes quite clear both by the omission of the passion of Peter and (by the omission) of the journey of Paul, who traveled to Spain from the city (of Rome).

The canon list juxtaposes Paul's travel to Spain with Peter's martyrdom, but does not mention Paul's death. While it cannot be demonstrated that its author knew these items from a single source, or indeed from any written source, it is likely that the compiler meant to compare the Lukan Acts with another document rather than with oral tradition. The *Acts of Peter*, in a form that included material about Paul, is the likely source of this association (Schmidt, 1903: 105–6; 1926: 495; cf. Vouaux, 1922: 110–13). Schmidt even argued that specific details of the wording show use of the *Acts of Peter* (1903: 105). If, as others have argued, the list belongs to the fourth century, Paul's trip to Spain and the manner of Peter's death would have been widely known, but it would be very surprising that Paul's martyrdom is not mentioned alongside Peter's. Schneemelcher is skeptical that any relationship with the *Acts of Peter* can be demonstrated (1992a: 272).

Jan Bremmer (1998b: 17) has suggested that the imagery of the demonic adversary in Perpetua's dream in the *Martyrdom of Perpetua* derives from Marcellus's dream in AcPetVerc 22:9–19. If so, this would prove the presence of the text in Carthage by the first years of the third century. On a later dating of the *Acts of Peter*, the influence could go in the other direction. Allusions to the stories of the speaking dog and infant in Commodian's *Carmen apologeticum* (text and commentary in Salvatore, 1977) may indicate that the *Acts of Peter* was known in North Africa near the middle of the third century, or a little later (Schmidt, 1903: 106–7).

Similarities to both the *Acts of Paul* and the *Acts of John* indicate that the *Acts of Peter* belongs relatively early in the sequence of apocryphal acts, but the nature, extent, and direction of dependence are all still under discussion (see below). The *Acts of Peter* was almost certainly used by the *Acts of Andrew* (MacDonald, 1997: 33–35), and the *Acts of Thomas*, both written in the early third century. Because Tertullian's comment on the recent composition of the *Acts of Paul* (*De bapt.* 17.3) provides the best external evidence for the dating of any of the apocryphal acts, efforts to establish the date of composition for the *Acts of Peter* have centered on the question of its relationship to the *Acts of Paul*. Those who consider the *Acts of Peter* dependent on the *Acts of Paul* have generally dated the *Acts of Peter* to the last decades of the second century or early decades of the third century (Vouaux, 1922: 52–53, 203–6). Poupon suggests that the original text was composed around 200 c.e., and the revisions made two or three decades later (1988: 4381). However, if the *Acts of Peter* was used by the author of the *Acts of Paul*, the original composition should be dated before 190 c.e. (Schmidt, 1930: 154; Schmidt and Schubart, 1936: 127–30; Schneemelcher, 1992a: 283; see also Bremmer, 1998b: 17–18, though his reasons are different), perhaps as early as 170 (Thomas, 2003: 28, 39) or even 160 c.e. (Zahn, 1892: 2. 841). It is likely that the version of the *Acts of Paul* represented by the Hamburg papyrus made use of the *Acts of Peter*, but whether Tertullian knew the *Acts of Paul* in that form is far from certain.

The evidence is stronger that the Syrian *Didascalia* drew directly from the *Acts of Peter* around 260 c.e. in its depiction of Simon as a heretic (Schmidt, 1903: 147; 1926: 507; Vouaux, 1922: 119–21; Schneemelcher, 1992a: 273). It is more difficult to determine whether the basic writing (*Grundschrift*) behind the Pseudo-Clementine romances made use of the *Acts of Peter*, possibly in Syria at about the same time (see below).

Harnack (1911) and Schmidt (1903: 167–71) both argued that the *Acts of Peter* was known even outside of Christian circles in the later part of the third century. A quotation attributed to the philosopher Porphyry is preserved in the *Apocriticos* of Macarius Magnes (2.22; 4.5), in which Porphyry argues that Peter was in Rome only briefly before his execution. This chronology seems to agree with the *Acts of Peter* against later Roman tradition. However, his comment shows only that Porphyry, who had spent time in both Athens and Rome, was aware of competing traditions among Christians (Flamion, 1910: 9–10; Schneemelcher, 1992a: 273).

PLACE OF COMPOSITION

Uncertainty over the place of composition continues as well. The cities in which the events take place, Jerusalem and Rome, have each been proposed. Other evidence points to northern Asia Minor. Syria has also found an advocate (Poupon, 1997: 1043). The argument for Jerusalem rests on the hypothesis that the lost Jerusalem section employed local traditions. Schmidt was impressed with the accurate designation of the city gate leading toward Neapolis, yet he had to admit that this information might have been be found elsewhere (1903: 110–11). The nomenclature belongs to the period after the destruction of the city in 70 c.e., so that any tradition behind the story was probably formed well after Peter's activity there. Because the *Acts of Peter* refers to Peter's twelve-year stay in Jerusalem (ch. 5), it probably contained additional narratives located in that city, but there is no evidence that it preserved early traditions about Peter's activity there. The note that Peter and Paul confronted Simon together in Jerusalem (AcPetVerc 23:14) is probably a modification of the story found in Acts 8:14.

Most of the surviving narrative takes place in Rome, but the extent the author's knowledge of Roman landmarks is debated. Schmidt pointed to the plausibility of placing a public disputation in the Julian forum (1903: 109–10). Ficker countered by questioning the author's knowledge of the relationship between the *Via sacra* and the Julian forum. Ficker also pointed to the author's incomplete understanding of the distinctive relationship between the city and its ports (1903: 35–36). The image of the city's believers gathering in a single house suggests that the author knew little of Roman Christianity at any period.

Schmidt also suggested that the strong interest in forgiveness found in the *Acts of Peter* was characteristic of Rome, and that the text belonged in the line between the *Shepherd of Hermas* and Callistus (1903: 100). However, the *Acts of Peter* is still a long way from the position of Callistus. Peter does not presume to grant forgiveness; he only intercedes on behalf of repentant sinners. Rome did not have an exclusive claim on the issue of forgiveness (Ficker, 1903: 41–42). Other elements of the *Acts of Peter* conflict with known Roman traditions. Justin Martyr, writing in Rome in the 160s, may have been the first to believe that Simon Magus had come to Rome, but he does not associate Simon's activity there with Peter. As noted above, Hippolytus offers a significantly different account of Simon's demise. *First Clement* already brings Peter and Paul together as Roman martyrs. Later, they are pictured as having been in the city at the same time and as having been martyred either on the same day or exactly one year apart. The *Acts of Peter* does not link the two martyrdoms so closely. The failure clearly to specify the location of Peter's martyrdom, along with the critique of Marcellus's burial honors for the apostle (AcPetMart 11[40]:3–7), seem to conflict with Roman interests in the narrative, but they are not sharply enough focused to constitute a polemic against cultic honors for Peter. In any case, an argument for a Roman provenance requires an early date of composition, since the Vatican Hill was marked as the site of Peter's martyrdom by the end of the second century.

Others have argued that the *Acts of Peter* was more likely to have been written in Asia Minor. (Ficker, 1903: 43–44; 1924: 229; Bremmer, 1998b: 14–16). The extensive similarities with the *Acts of Paul* are one reason for doing so. The two apostles enjoy prominent roles in the canonical book of Acts, which was probably written in this region. Ficker offered a number of additional observations to support his view. He suggested that the Hospice of the Bithynians mentioned in AcPetVerc 4:15 might reflect local interests. The most intriguing of Ficker's suggestions is the possible connection between the senator Marcellus of the *Acts of Peter* and M. Granius Marcellus, praetor and then governor of Bithynia in 15 C.E. This Marcellus was prosecuted on charges of treason (*maiestas*) when one of his underlings reported that he had spoken disrespectfully of Tiberius and had replaced the head on a statue of Augustus with a portrait of the new emperor. The historical Marcellus was also charged with extortion (*repetundia*) in connection with his service as governor in Bithynia. The combination of the name with charges involving both misuse of a provincial office and an offense against an imperial statue is striking. Ficker suggests that Christian tradition granted the historical figure a posthumous conversion by a process similar to the one which brought Queen Tryphaena into the *Acts of Paul* (1903: 44–45). Ficker argues that this is most likely to have happened in Bithynia (1903: 39). However, the story was widely known; Tacitus cites Marcellus's trial as an example of Tiberius's growing abuse of power (*Annals*, 1.74). Bremmer has argued that interest in Christianity among the senatorial class may have arisen earlier in Asia Minor than in Rome, especially after the ranks of senators were greatly expanded in the later part of the second century (1998b: 17–18).

Our knowledge of early Christianity in northern Asia Minor is limited. The canonical Acts rather pointedly removes the region from the sphere of

Paul's missionary activity (Acts 16:7), while 1 Pet 1:1 links Peter to the region. Writing in the early years of the second century from Bithynia, Pliny the Younger shows that already in the first decades of the second century religious competition was an issue, that Christians were to be found in every social class (*ordo*), and that many Christians were willing to abandon their new faith when pressure was applied (*Letters* 10.96). A generation or so later, Marcion came out of this region. A little later still, Alexander of Abononteichos established the dramatically successful cult of Glykon, the new Asclepius, in Paphlagonia. Finally, Montanism got its start in the neighboring region of Phrygia. Clearly, Christians in northern and central Asia Minor had known persecution and competition, either of which might lead to apostasy.

The letters written by bishop Dionysios of Corinth to churches in the region show that questions engaged by the *Acts of Peter* were actively discussed around 170 C.E., a time of renewed persecution. Dionysios urges moderation on the question of marriage, he comments on the interpretation of scripture, and argues for the reception of apostates as well as those who have suffered moral lapses (Eusebius *Hist. eccl.* 4.23.6).

The most likely home of the *Acts of Peter* is then somewhere on the axis between Rome and northern Asia Minor. It is possible that a provincial composed the text in Rome, but it is more likely that someone with a little knowledge of Rome wrote in the east. There a senator like Marcellus might be expected to act as a patron to the provincials, even though the text makes him the patron of provincial Christians in Rome. In either case, concern for *peregrini* (provincials who were not citizens) would have been less important after the general grant of citizenship by Caracalla in 212 C.E.

In summary, neither external nor internal evidence is sufficient to settle the questions of the dating, provenance, and authorship of the *Acts of Peter*. It is most probable that the it was composed in the last third of the second century by an author or authors who cannot now be identified. Northern Asia Minor is the most likely place of composition. The Latin translation found in the Vercelli codex was originally made in the fourth century (Bremmer, 1998b: 19), probably in North Africa (Poupon, 1998), or perhaps in Spain (Baldwin, 2005: 181–93).

THEOLOGICAL CONCERNS

The issues prominent in the *Acts of Peter* are ones that challenged Christian communities in the second half of the second century and for many years thereafter. The intense competition for adherents presupposed by the *Acts of Peter* was widespread in the Roman Empire at this time. Christianity had to compete not only with long established civic and domestic cults but also with Hellenized versions of oriental religions, with newly established cults, such as that of Glykon, and with various forms of popular philosophy offering guidelines for living the good life. In the fluid situation of the second century, even Antinous, the young companion of the emperor Hadrian, received divine honors from a number of cities. Lucian's lampoon of Peregrinus shows how actively Christianity was engaged in this competition among cults. Both Alexander of Abononteichos and Peregrinus have much in common with the figure of Simon Magus as he is portrayed in the *Acts of Peter*. In fact, Lucian describes how Alexander made a point of excluding Christians and accused them of spreading slanders against him.

When Peter reaches Rome, he announces that he will confront Simon with both words and deeds in order to show that he, Peter, is the messenger of the true God (AcPetVerc 7:25). The theological ideas presented by the apostle are neither fully developed nor rigorously consistent. Throughout the *Acts of Peter*, sin is associated with ignorance while salvation is equated with illumination, but the text should not be considered gnostic in either a technical or nontechnical sense. Rather, a moderate version of middle-Platonic, qualified dualism is presupposed. While the spiritual realm is considered superior, it is not wholly disconnected from the physical realm. Physical sight and blindness can be pointers to spiritual light or lack of it. With insight, the physical world becomes transparent to the spiritual.

In consequence of this, most of the miracles recorded are meant to direct attention to a higher reality, God, but they are also meant to be taken seriously as concrete aid to their recipients (Stoops, 1986). At times, a group of witnesses will report seeing Christ in different forms at the same time (AcPetVerc 20:24; 21:12–15). In some assessments, these polymorphic appearances of Christ are said to be associated with a docetic Christology—the assertion that Christ merely appeared in human form without becoming genuinely human. However, the *Acts of Peter* insists on the physical reality of Jesus. The motif of polymorphism is used to assert Christ's accessibility to all in a form appropriate to each (Cartlidge, 1986: 63). The Christology of the *Acts of Peter* is more monarchian (subsuming the existence Christ, the Son, within that of God the Father) than docetic (Pervo, 1997: 48). Only Peter's speeches at and from the cross speak of fully escaping from a world that is ultimately to be judged deficient. These speeches, which may in any case derive from a different tradition, are presented as a higher form of spiritual knowledge.

J. Flamion argued that the theological and christological inconsistencies found in the *Acts of Peter* reflect the inherent tensions between the kind of assertions found in the Roman "Symbol" (the early creed) and the influences of a popular Platonizing philosophy. In the *Acts of Peter*, these tensions are allowed to stand without resolution (Flamion, 1909: 245–77). Westra (1998) has argued that the creedal elements incorporated into Peter's speeches have their closest parallels in the *regulae fidei* of the second century—commonly associated with Irenaeus of Lyon—insofar as they do not distinguish clearly between God and Christ and do not give the Holy Spirit a significant role most of the time. Many of the arguments that the *Acts of Peter* brings to bear in defending Christianity resemble those found in Justin's apologetic writings. Like Justin, the author of the *Acts of Peter* treats the fulfillment of Old Testament prophecy in the career of Jesus as an important demonstration of the truth of Christianity. Like Justin, the *Acts of Peter* sees demonic forces at work behind competing forms of cult and heresy (*1 Apol.* 14; 21; 26; 56–58). The most striking common feature is the story of a statue raised in honor of Simon Magus in Rome (Justin *1 Apol.* 26.2; AcPetVerc 10:6). Indeed, Schmidt was convinced that Justin served as a source for the *Acts of Peter* (1903: 88–89). On the whole, the author of the *Acts of Peter* seems less well informed about, or less interested in, the historical Simon than Justin was. The author is certainly less informed than Hippolytus. More importantly, the author lacks Justin's confidence in the efficacy of theoretical arguments and resorts to miracle stories as the primary means of addressing the threat of competition.

Miracles similar to those that play an important of the *Acts of Peter* are found in the propaganda for many contemporary cults as well as in the romances and the lives of philosophers. The miracles resulting from Peter's prayers are intended to show that faith in Christ is the best way to procure benefits in this world as well as in the spiritual realm. One of the ways Christ provides for believers is through aiding the wealthy and influential, thereby motivating them to support the poor among the faithful. Lucian's account of Alexander of Abonoteichos shows how important the patronage of a senator could be for the practical success of a new religious organization. In the *Acts of Peter*, the stories of Marcellus and Chryse reveal the author's anxious efforts to tap those resources while limiting the influence of those donors in spiritual matters (Stoops, 1986).

The favor shown to Peter and other believers by Roman elites has complicated attempts to date the text. Harnack held that the conversions among the senatorial class depicted in the *Acts of Peter* were not plausible before the middle of the third century. Schmidt ultimately followed C. Erbes's argument that significant interest in Christianity among the Roman elite was plausible during the reign of Septimius Severus (1930: 154). Needless to say, some latitude must be allowed for imaginative reconstruction of the apostolic period; the canonical Acts already depicted Roman officials as well disposed toward Christianity.

A further complicating factor is that Christianity itself was far from unified in the second and third centuries. Various groups, among them "orthodox," Marcionites, Valentinians, and Simonians, actively competed against each other in many parts of the empire. The fact that Simon has no clearly defined theology in the *Acts of Peter* suggests, therefore, that the author was not primarily interested in doctrinal disputes. In comparison, the figures of Cleobis and Simon in the *Acts of Paul* articulate a much clearer set of theological propositions, and their areas of disagreement with Paul are precisely defined. Similarly, in the Pseudo-Clementine literature the conflict between

Peter and Simon includes extensive theological debates. The *Acts of Peter* is more concerned with promoting faith understood as trust and loyalty. It focuses on illumination and repentance rather than on dogmatic or metaphysical precision.

The recurring issue of the forgiveness of sin is closely linked to winning back those who have faltered or even left the faith. Peter points to himself as one who received mercy in spite of his earlier failings. In AcPetVerc 28:52, the apostle is made to say that repentance is possible even for Simon, who had by now been identified as the messenger of Satan (17:56, 32:21). Similarly, Rufina, who suffers paralysis when she approaches the eucharist in a state of impurity, is told that forgiveness is possible if she repents (2:6). This story leads to a speech in which Paul assures the wavering believers in Rome that their sins can also be forgiven; this is followed by a prayer in which the apostle asks God and Christ to do just that.

This openness toward the forgiveness of sins, even those committed after baptism, is paralleled by the text's moderate views on asceticism. The apostles and others fast on occasions of prayer (AcPetVerc 1:5; 5:1, 11; 17:8; 18:1), and Peter fasts in preparation for confronting Simon (22:6). But there are no other discussions of diet. The eucharist consists of bread (AcPetBG 2:27; AcPetVerc 5:30) or bread and water (AcPetVerc 2:1), but no special meaning is attached to the absence of wine. Chastity is taken for granted, but it does not stand at the center of the apostle's message and is never closely identified with salvation. The attitude toward sexuality does not go much beyond what is advocated by Paul. Marriage and procreation are not rejected out of hand. In fact, normal marriage relations are challenged only in cases where excessive lust is the issue as with Ptolemy in the Coptic "Act of Peter" (AcPetBG 1:22; 2:7) and Albinus in the *Martyrdom* (AcPetMart 5[34]:3–4). Adultery and concubinage are clearly rejected, but virtually all Christians in the second or third centuries would agree on that. To cite Dionysios of Corinth again, Eusebius reports that

> [In a] letter to Knossos, [Dionysios] asks Pinytos, the bishop residing there, not to place a heavy burden on the brothers and sisters requiring chastity and to consider the weakness of the many. To this Pinytos replied that he admired and welcomed Dionysius, but asked him in turn to provide sometime more solid food, and to nourish the people with him with another more advanced letter, so that they might not be fed on milky words through their whole lives and grow to old age unaware and still treated as children. (Hist. eccl. 4.23.6)

Eusebius makes it clear that his sympathies lie with Pinytos, but the author of the *Acts of Peter* would have sided with Dionysios. Except for the question of concubinage, the values advocated in the *Acts of Peter* are not radically different from those professed, if not always practiced, by the elites of Roman society. Yves Tissot has pointed out that the issue of purity raised in the *Martyrdom* has more to do with the conventions of martyrdom stories than with encratism (1998: 114–16).

More striking, though perhaps related, is the absence of persecution at the hands of Roman officials outside Paul's brief incarceration and Peter's actual martyrdom. The primary "persecutor" in the *Acts of Peter* is Simon (AcPetVerc 6:33; 7:2; 22:6; 28:51), who seduces believers away from Christ. Peter is threatened by the crowd (28:32–34), but they are equally willing to attack Simon (28:45–49, 32:13), so the issue is not Peter's status as a Christian. This attitude suggests that the *Acts of Peter* was written in a period of relative calm. The early years of the reign of Marcus Aurelius were such a period for Christians. Peace returned to the churches during the reigns of Commodus and Septimius Severus.

The leading concerns of the *Acts of Peter* find parallels in Justin Martyr and Dionysios of Corinth, that is, in the period between 160 and 170 c.e. The familiar figures of Marcion, Alexander of Abonoteichos, and Peregrinus are sufficient to account for the character of Simon. In fact, many elements in the *Acts of Peter* could be understood as responses to the success of Marcionite Christians. Peter seems to provide a firmer grounding in faith than Paul. Peter employs Old Testament prophets in his exposition of Christianity and appears to favor the Gospels of Matthew and John over Luke. Peter preaches a merciful God, who is clearly both creator of the world and the father of the Christ. We even find a wealthy ship's captain, although after being converted and baptized by Peter this captain disappears into the mass of believers. Marcellus's unsteady patronage of believers could reflect Marcion's donations to Roman Christians. While these features do not add up to a clear polemic against Marcion, Marcion's career, no less than that of Alexander of Abonoteichos, confirms that the issues addressed in the *Acts of Peter* were matters of debate in the second half of the second century. The figure of Simon Magus provided a convenient foil for addressing all of these concerns.

The absence of general persecution, the lack of clear engagement with the Montanist crisis, together with the paucity of fixed traditions concerning Peter's martyrdom, all point away from a later date. When arguing for a third century date, Schmidt suggested that the *Acts of Peter* was written to oppose Montanist tendencies emerging in the author's circle of knowledge or influence (1903: 111). But the fact that the author is comfortable with prophetic dogs and infants makes this unlikely. It is more probable that the *Acts of Peter* belonged to the kind of church that the Montanist movement later reacted against. The rise of Montanism and the increase in persecution during the reign of M. Aurelius could explain the stronger dualism, increased asceticism, and greater conflict with society found in the other apocryphal acts (see M. Sordi [1986: 70–74] for the effect of Marcus Aurelius on attitudes toward Christian participation in society). Taken together, the evidence points to a date of composition between 160 and 175 c.e. It is not necessary to connect either the initial composition or a later level of redaction to the Decian persecution and the related controversy over the readmission of lapsed Christians. It is, however, easy to see why the *Acts of Peter* would have attracted interest at that time.

RELATIONSHIP TO
OTHER EARLY
CHRISTIAN LITERATURE

The *Acts of Peter* treats the Old Testament as authoritative, and Peter employs quotations from it in apologetic arguments based on the fulfillment of prophecy. The author probably relied on a testimony collection rather than on the full texts. Turner noted the abbreviation of Isa 7:13 in the AcPetVerc 24:6 (1931: 129). The *Acts of Peter* also shows knowledge of a number of New Testament works, but only the sayings of Jesus, including extracanonical sayings quoted in AcPetVerc 10:14 and 38:8, are treated as authoritative (Stoops, 1994: 403–4; 1997: 65–71; Thomas, 1997: 194). The scene in AcPetVerc 20:5–8 presupposes that gospel-like texts were used in worship, but emphasizes the need for interpretation. The "living word" of oral tradition seems still to carry more authority. The author apparently knew most if not all of the New Testament gospels. The raising of the widow's son (AcPetVerc 25:6–17; 27: 1–10) echoes Luke 7:11–14, but in general the Gospel of Matthew is favored. At least some of Paul's letters were known as well, particularly Romans and First Corinthians. They are not cited as scripture, but many names are borrowed and Pauline phrases inform the rhetoric of the *Acts of Peter*, especially in the sections in which Paul is present (Thomas, 1997: 189–90).

The canonical Acts of the Apostles influenced the author, but where the *Acts of Peter* most clearly overlaps canonical Acts it does not follow the Lukan Acts in detail (Matthews, 1997: 208–14; Stoops, 1994; Thomas, 1997: 195–98). Peter's encounter with Simon takes place in Jerusalem rather than in Samaria, and includes Paul rather than Philip (AcPetVerc 23: 14–16). Paul's imprisonment in Rome appears as background for his departure for Spain, a journey that is not mentioned in the canonical Acts (but see Rom 15:24, 28). The hypothesis that the *Acts of Peter* was intended to continue or complete the Lukan Acts is less plausible than the alternative, that a more extensive original was truncated to follow on the Pseudo-Clementine *Recognitions* in composite manuscripts.

Narrative parallels are, of course, especially rich in the other major apocryphal acts. Many theological motifs are also shared, but the nature and direction of dependence is not always clear. Schmidt considered overlapping traditions to be evidence of the author's lack of imagination (Schmidt and Schubart, 1936: 129–30). Over against this judgment, it must be insisted that developing the skills of imitation and variation were among the chief goals of rhetorical education. The authors of apocryphal acts may not have been highly trained, but their procedures were not necessarily different in kind from those of writers with greater skill. Ancient attitudes toward the use of texts, and the continued circulation of oral traditions, make it particularly difficult to reach certainty on questions of dependence, literary or otherwise, among the apocryphal acts (Perkins, 1993; Valantasis, 1992). The *Acts of Peter* may have been used by the author of the *Acts of Paul* and the author of the *Acts of John* in Asia Minor. It was almost certainly used later by the authors of *Acts of Andrew* in Greece and *Acts of Thomas* in Syria.

ACTS OF PAUL

The quantity of material common to the *Acts of Peter* and the *Acts of Paul* is sufficient to convince most scholars that the two documents are literarily related. Schmidt, who was deeply engaged with both texts, initially defended the priority of the *Acts of Paul*. He argued that the motif of "the household of Caesar," which plays a major role in motivating the martyrdom of Paul, is introduced gratuitously in AcPetMart 12(41). The *Acts of Peter* also refers to Paul's execution without narrating it. Schmidt supposed that the *Acts of Peter* had borrowed the *Quo vadis* scene from the *Acts of Paul*, where Origen said it was to be found (1903: 84). Dennis Ronald MacDonald argues for the priority of *Acts of Paul* on similar grounds (1997: 13–24). But the motif of the imperial household in the AcPetVerc 3 and AcPetMart 12(41) may be derived directly from Phil 4:22 rather than the *Acts of Paul*. The most important parallel among those MacDonald cites is the use of the verb δραπετύειν, "to run away or desert." The military meaning found in the *Acts of Paul* is not required in the *Martyrdom of Peter*, where the more general sense of running away from a duty fits the context better. Further, the *Acts of Peter* does not exploit the imagery of Christ's kingship or make much use of the military metaphor for loyalty. If the *Acts of Paul* is the source of this motif, its softening in the *Acts of Peter* needs to be explained. While the *Acts of Peter* does mention Paul's martyrdom under Nero (AcPetVerc 1:15), it does not go beyond traditions that were well known by the beginning of the second century. It shows no direct knowledge of the *Martyrdom of Paul*.

Schmidt reversed his judgment as to priority after finding a version of the *Quo vadis* scene in the Hamburg papyrus of the *Acts of Paul* (Schmidt, 1930: 152; Schmidt and Schubart, 1936: 127–30). Schmidt argued that Christ's words to Paul, "I am going to be crucified again," are inappropriate there because Paul suffers decapitation rather than crucifixion. This argument, by itself, is insufficient to settle the matter; possible use of metaphor must be allowed. Even apart from Paul's own language of being crucified with Christ (Gal 2:20), the "new crucifixion" to be suffered by Christ could refer to the apostasy in Rome (cf. Heb 6:6).

It is important to observe that the two scenes function differently. In the *Acts of Paul,* Christ is to be crucified *in the person of* the apostle and guides Paul to Rome. In the *Acts of Peter,* Christ comes to Rome to be crucified again *in place of* the apostle, who is fleeing. When Peter comes to his senses, Christ returns to heaven. MacDonald finds this sequence awkward at best (1997: 18). On the other hand, story elements that MacDonald sees as "draconian" have parallels in *Mart. Pol. 5.* Polycarp also debates whether he should leave the city in order to escape arrest and prolong his service to the community. He goes into hiding, but then has a vision which foreshadows the manner of his martyrdom. In both cases the details reinforce the linkage between the martyrdom of the saint and the passion of Christ.

Paul's voyage from Corinth to Rome (P.Hamb. 6–7), which provides the setting for the *Quo vadis* vision, employs many elements that appear to be derived from the two apostolic voyages in AcPetVerc 1–6. Paul's preparations in the *Acts of Paul* closely parallel the events surrounding his departure for Spain in AcPetVerc 3. His actual voyage is similar to Peter's journey to Rome in AcPetVerc 5. Most importantly, the *Acts of Paul* mentions that Peter had converted the captain of Paul's ship. Dismissing this note as a gloss (see Poupon, 1988: 4381) does not address the issue of the long series of narrative parallels to the *Acts of Peter* found in Paul's journey to Rome in the *Acts of Paul* (Stoops, 1992: 225–30). Deciding which text seems to make the most natural use of a particular motif does not settle the question of priority. That "better fit" could be a sign of originality or of secondary refinement (MacDonald, 1997: 13). Dependence may be no more than familiarity with the text; it is not necessary to imagine that one author worked from an open copy of the other text. In the case of the apostolic voyages and the *Quo vadis* scene, I believe that in this sense at least priority should be assigned to the *Acts of Peter.* The alternative, favored by Vouaux (1922: 28), Poupon (1988: 4369–72) and Thomas (2003: 21–29), is that the original *Acts of Peter* was expanded with material borrowed from the *Acts of Paul.*

The episode in Myra (P.Heid. 28–35) also shares a number of motifs with the *Acts of Peter.* The text is fragmentary but appears to have been packed with miracle story motifs. The presence of numerous features familiar from the New Testament gospels' miracle stories in this section of the *Acts of Paul* suggests that it is secondary. There is no reason for the author of the *Acts of Peter* to have dropped them. On balance, it appears that at least some parts of the *Acts of Paul* are dependent on the *Acts of Peter* in a version that included the first three chapters of the Vercelli *Acts.*

ACTS OF JOHN

Junod and Kaestli also see a close relationship between the *Acts of Peter* and the *Acts of John.* Their argument for the priority of the *Acts of John* is based on their judgment that its heterodox character and the relative lack of New Testament divine titles indicate an early date (1983: 695). This argument has not convinced everyone. The clearest parallels between the *Acts of Peter* and the *Acts of John* are the connections each makes between the transfiguration scene and the broader notion of polymorphism, and the lists of christological titles. In AcJohn 87, Drusina reports that Christ appeared to her in the form of the apostle. John explains to the crowd that it has always been impossible fully to communicate the significance of the things he has seen and heard. He then relates several stories concerning polymorphic appearances of Christ. John's second account of the transfiguration (AcJohn 91) gives both John himself and polymorphism larger roles than they have in AcPetVerc 20. The combination of the transfiguration—that is, the ineffability of its true meaning—with a broader polymorphism suggests some kind of connection exists between the two apostolic acts. The author of the *Acts of John* may have wanted to offer a competing version of the traditions in which Peter plays the more prominent role (see MacDonald 1992: 624–25; Pervo, 1997: 49).

Junod and Kaestli have argued that the *Acts of John* is the earliest of the apocryphal acts, in part because it gives the greatest emphasis to polymorphism. It employs the motif for theological purposes, to show the incomprehensible nature of God and God's accommodation to human need, in a manner similar to the *Acts of Peter*. It also uses the theme for dramatic escape sequences similar to those found in the *Acts of Paul*, the *Acts of Andrew*, and the *Acts of Thomas*. They conclude that the *Acts of John* is the source for both kinds of use in the other apocryphal acts (1983: 699–700). MacDonald's contention that the *Acts of John* draws from both the *Acts of Paul* and the *Acts of Peter* is more plausible (1997: 24–32).

AcJohn 98 applies to the cross names which are usually found as christological titles; many are prominent in the Gospel of John. A similar list appears in the AcPetVerc 20, where they remain titles of Christ. The list in the *Acts of Peter* contains several additional titles that appear to be derived from parables of the synoptic tradition. Peter's speech in AcPetVerc 38–39 probably contributed to the discussion of the cross in AcJohn 99 as well (Schmidt, 1903: 97–99). The scene in which Cleopatra resurrects her husband (AcJohn 24) contains parallels to the resurrection by the prefect in AcPetVerc 26 and the reaction of the crowd in AcPetVerc 29. The use of the saying, "Do not return evil for evil," to hold out the possibility of conversion to even the most depraved of characters (AcJohn 81; AcPetVerc 28:50) is too general to establish a literary relationship. The same is true for the departure scene in AcJohn 58, which has some motifs in common with both AcPetVerc 2–4 and the *Acts of Paul* text preserved in P.Hamb. 6–7. Although the evidence is not conclusive, the dependence of the *Acts of John* on the *Acts of Peter* seems the less bold hypothesis. Resolution of the dependence question must await a clear decision on the text-history of the *Acts of John* (Lalleman, 1998: 166–77; Pervo, 1997: 53, 55).

Schneemelcher denies any literary dependence between the *Acts of Peter* and the *Acts of John*, arguing that widespread Christian traditions have been used in different ways in each of the two texts (1992a: 275). Long ago, Flamion argued a similar position more extensively. He suggested that both authors were dealing with the tensions between the church's emerging creed and Platonic philosophy. While the *Acts of Peter* lets these tensions stand, the *Acts of John* goes further in the Platonizing direction (Flamion, 1909: 251). This analysis may be the best way of understanding the differences in theological perspective seen in the two acts, but it does not account for the numerous parallels in specific details.

ACTS OF ANDREW

In his study of the *Acts of Andrew*, Jean-Marc Prieur has suggested that the author of *Acts of Andrew* knew an early version of the *Acts of Peter*. Prieur has noted a number of parallels between the *Acts of Andrew* and the *Acts of Peter*, especially in the martyrdoms (Prieur, 1989: 385–403). The speech addressed to the apostle's cross followed by an exhortation from the cross is structurally parallel to the *Acts of Peter*, although the comparison with Adam appears in a different context. Because the lack of New Testament christological titles is part of his argument for the early dating of the *Acts of Andrew*, Prieur suggests that the author of the *Acts of Andrew* might have known an early form of the *Acts of Peter* which lacked the numerous biblical references now found in its speeches (1989: 1. 402–3). The main support for this idea is his hypothesis as to the date of the *Acts of Andrew* and the theory formulated by Junod and Kaestli, in their study of the *Acts of John*, that early sources are likely to be less orthodox in their outlook than later ones (1983: 698–700). No manuscript evidence for such an early form of the *Acts of Peter* survives. MacDonald points to additional parallels to the *Acts of Peter* in the travel sections of the *Acts of Andrew and Matthias*, which he argues is part of the original *Acts of Andrew* (1990: 28–31; 1997: 33–35).

ACTS OF THOMAS

The author of the *Acts of Thomas* appears to have borrowed a number of elements from the *Acts of Peter* and placed them in new contexts (MacDonald, 1997: 33–35). King Gundafar in the second act has much in common with the senator Marcellus. The story told by the young man in Act 3 is similar to that told by Nikostratus in AcPetVerc 28:66–68. The serpent's self-identification in Act 3 (AcThom 32:1–16) and Thomas's speech to the demon in Act 5 (AcThom 44:1–6) both borrow language from Peter's speech in AcPetVerc 8:15–32. In Act 4, the death of a colt is said to be expedient for it (AcThom 41:4–7), a motif found in the story of Peter's daughter (1:15–16). The speaking animals found in the *Acts of Thomas* are not necessarily modeled on the speaking dog in Ac-PetVerc 9:9–15. The motif was widespread (Matthews, 1999; Spittler, 2008). The story of Rufina (AcPetVerc 2:2–8) may be the model for the withering eucharist at the beginning of Act 6 (AcThom 51:1–6). The divine aid given to Manashar in Act 13 (AcThom 154:8–10) is similar to the healing of the widow in AcPetVerc 20:2–4.

PSEUDO-CLEMENTINES

The Pseudo-Clementine *Homilies* and *Recognitions* are structured around a competition similar to the one which dominates the *Acts of Peter*, but the emphasis has shifted. The adventures of Clement's family provide a larger context for the confrontations between Peter and Simon. Theological debate plays a much larger role. Simon is given a more fully articulated position, and Peter becomes the mouthpiece for extensive theological speculation. Miracles play a supporting role. The so-called Basic Document behind the Pseudo-Clementines may have been constructed to fit between the Jerusalem and Roman sections of the *Acts of Peter*, but this is not likely (Schneemelcher, 1992a: 273–74). In the Pseudo-Clementines, Peter travels from Caesarea to Antioch, but the *Acts of Peter* seems to have Peter stay in Jerusalem for twelve years and then pursue Simon in Rome. The *Recognitions* did, however, come to be closely associated with the *Acts of Peter* in the manuscript tradition (Baldwin, 2005: 119–25; see further Jones [1982] for the complexities associated with the Pseudo-Clementine literature).

LATER DISTRIBUTION AND INFLUENCE

After the time of Eusebius the *Acts of Peter* became widely known, frequently in forms that included material dealing with Paul and the story of Peter's daughter. The single vellum leaf of P.Oxy. 849 is the earliest physical trace of the *Acts of Peter*. It shows that text was present in Egypt by the early fourth century in a form similar to the Vercelli Acts. P.Berol. 8502, which contains the Coptic "Act of Peter," probably dates from the early fifth century. The Syriac *Teaching of Simon Cephas in the City of Rome*, written in the fourth or fifth century, made use of elements of Peter's contest in the forum. The various translations of the *Martyrdom of Peter* show that it continued to serve as a liturgical text much longer in the east than in areas dominated by Rome.

The broad distribution of the *Acts of Peter* may have been due in part to its use among Manicheans. In *C. Adim.* 17.5, Augustine cites what appears to be a version of the *Acts of Peter* as a text valued among Manicheans. While the existence of a Manichean collection of apostolic acts has been questioned (Kaestli, 1997; Baldwin, 2005: 98), Peter Nagel has argued that a collection of acts was used by Herakleides near the beginning of the fourth century. The

Manichean *Psalm Book* dating from the mid-fourth century seems to know all five of the "Leucian" Acts. Knut Schäferdiek has argued that all five acts had been translated into Latin by Manichaeans before the end of the fourth century (1992a: 92). The dualistic potential of parts of the *Acts of Peter* was perhaps sufficient to have made it interesting to Manicheans (Poupon, 1988: 4366; Schneemelcher, 1992a: 278), but it should be noted that only a few motifs from it found their way into the Manichean *Psalm Book* (Schäferdiek, 1992: 88–90). Manichaean use may also lie behind the Sogdian fragment containing a version of the story in AcPetVerc 28 and 31 (Müller, 1934: 528–31, 603). The same elements of dualism and sexual restraint would have made the *Acts of Peter* attractive to the author of the Pseudo-Titus *Epistle on Virginity*, who was probably a Priscillianist writing in Spain during the fifth century (Santos Otero, 1992b: 54). The Pseudo-Titus epistle alludes to the story of Rufina (AcPetVerc 2:2–8) and provides the only surviving version of the story of the gardener's daughter cited by Augustine.

The *Acts of Peter* seems to have been known in Asia Minor in a more complete form as well. The *Life of Abercius*, composed in the mid-fourth century, borrows passages from Peter's speeches in AcPetVerc 7, 20, and 21 for use against the Manicheans. It also employs part of Paul's speech in AcPetVerc 2 (text in Nissen, 1912; see also Nissen, 1908, 190–203; 1912; Baldwin, 2005: 197–241 with text and translation of the parallel passages). The *Acts of Philip* (see Amsler et al, 1996), written in the fourth or fifth century probably in Phrygian Hierapolis, includes a brief report of the story of Peter's daughter along with materials from chs. 28 and 38 of the *Acts of Peter*.

For the Roman church, the original *Acts of Peter* was gradually supplanted by versions that more closely linked the deaths of Peter and Paul. The Pseudo-Linus *Passion of Peter* from late fourth-century Rome (Thomas, 2003: 123 n.73) elaborates on the Greek *Martyrdom of Peter*, and circulated together with the *Passion of Paul* created on the basis of the martyrdom from the *Acts of Paul*. The Pseudo-Hegessipus *De excidio Hierosolymitano*, composed around 370 c.e., employs material from the contest in the forum and Peter's martyrdom, including a version of the *Quo vadis* scene (3.2). Simon is presented as a friend of Nero, and Paul is brought into the story, though with few details. The two apostles suffer martyrdom on the same day. The text reflects Roman interests but may have been written in North Africa. It was followed by the Pseudo-Marcellus texts, the *Passion of Peter and Paul* (from the second half of the sixth century; Flamion, 1910: 687), and the *Acts of Peter and Paul* (in the seventh century; Flamion, 1910: 688–89). The *Acts of Nereus and Achilleus* uses a good deal of material from the *Acts of Peter*, including a greatly expanded version of the story of Peter's daughter (text in Achelis, 1893; discussion with translation of the parallel passages in Molinari, 2005: 61–80; see also Thomas, 2003: 45–46). The author, writing in Rome in the fifth or sixth century, still had access to a more complete form of the Greek *Acts of Peter* than is extant today, and may in addition have known the Pseudo-Linus *Passion* (Flamion, 1910: 450–53). Book 1 of the Pseudo-Abdias *Apostolic History*, possibly written in Gaul in the sixth century, also employs material from the *Acts of Peter*. The *Acts of Xanthippe and Polyxena*, another sixth-century text and of uncertain provenance, includes material from the *Acts of Peter* throughout; in particular, it makes extensive use of AcPetVerc 1–5 in its ch. 24 (James, 1893: 43–85).

The *Acts of Peter* thus influenced a broad range of later literature, both directly and through derivative texts such as the Pseudo-Linus and Pseudo-Marcellus martyrdoms (for information on these later texts, see Elliott, 1993: 427–30; Geerard, 1992: 109–12; and Santos Otero, 1992: 436–43). With the exception of the *Martyrdom*, the early *Acts of Peter* came very close to disappearing into the literature it inspired. Something similar happened in the visual arts. Most of the images of Peter in early Christian art present the apostle as a new Moses. Peter's martyrdom is usually portrayed with an arrest scene, and is associated with that of Paul—in agreement with the later versions (Cartlidge, 2001: 134–38, 162–71; Dinkler, 1939; Stuhlfauth, 1925). Indeed, David Cartlidge can isolate only a few scenes, including the speaking dog (AcPetVerc 9:9–15) and Peter reading to an audience (AcPetVerc 20:5–17), that are derived from the early version of the *Acts of Peter* (Cartlidge, 2001: 167–68).

BASIS OF THE TRANSLATION

The translation offered here is based on the editions of Lipsius and Léon Vouaux, and like them follows the Greek in the *Martyrdom*. The Latin of the manuscript has been followed where possible, which is not always the case. Other texts that appear to quote sections of the *Acts of Peter* directly, especially the *Life of Abercius*, have been followed where they seem to offer better readings. Turner's suggested emendations have all been considered. His suggestions are ingenious, but many yield readings which normalize the text in matters of theology as well as grammar. The readings offered by Baldwin (2005: *passim*) and Hilhorst (1998: 154–60) have also been considered. Minor emendations have not been noted. The translation of the Coptic "Act of Peter" (in the notes identified as AcPetBG) is based on Schmidt's original publication and the more recent editions by Brashler and Parrott and Roy. The extract from the Pseudo-Titus epistle and Codex Cambray are based on De Bruyne's publications of these texts. Gérard Poupon's notes to his translation of the *Acts of Peter* in the volume edited by Bovon and Geoltrain (1997) have also been considered. Poupon's critical edition of the *Acts of Peter* for the *Corpus Christianorum Series Apocryphorum* is eagerly awaited.

HOW TO USE THIS BOOK

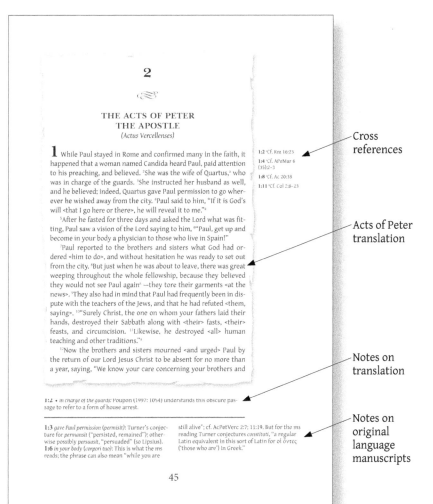

2

THE ACTS OF PETER
THE APOSTLE
(Actus Vercellenses)

1 While Paul stayed in Rome and confirmed many in the faith, it happened that a woman named Candida heard Paul, paid attention to his preaching, and believed. ²She was the wife of Quartus,ᵃ who was in charge of the guards. ³She instructed her husband as well, and he believed; indeed, Quartus gave Paul permission to go wherever he wished away from the city. ⁴Paul said to him, "If it is God's will <that I go here or there>, he will reveal it to me."ᵃ

⁵After he fasted for three days and asked the Lord what was fitting, Paul saw a vision of the Lord saying to him, ⁶"Paul, get up and become in your body a physician to those who live in Spain!"

⁷Paul reported to the brothers and sisters what God had ordered <him to do>, and without hesitation he was ready to set out from the city. ⁸But just when he was about to leave, there was great weeping throughout the whole fellowship, because they believed they would not see Paul againᵃ —they tore their garments <at the news>. ⁹They also had in mind that Paul had frequently been in dispute with the teachers of the Jews, and that he had refuted <them, saying>, ¹⁰ᵃ"Surely Christ, the one on whom your fathers laid their hands, destroyed their Sabbath along with <their> fasts, <their> feasts, and circumcision. ¹¹Likewise, he destroyed <all> human teaching and other traditions."ᵃ

¹²Now the brothers and sisters mourned <and urged> Paul by the return of our Lord Jesus Christ to be absent for no more than a year, saying, "We know your care concerning your brothers and

Cross references
1:2 ᶜCf. Rm 16:23
1:4 ᶜCf. APeMar 6 (35):2-3
1:8 ᶜCf. Ac 20:18
1:11 ᶜCf. Col 2:8-23

Acts of Peter translation

Notes on translation

1:2 • *in charge of the guards*: Poupon (1997: 1054) understands this obscure passage to refer to a form of house arrest.

Notes on original language manuscripts

1:3 *gave Paul permission (permisit)*: Turner's conjecture for *permansit* ("persisted, remained"); otherwise possibly *persuasit*, "persuaded" (so Lipsius). **1:6** *in your body (corpori tuo)*: This is what the ms reads; the phrase can also mean "while you are still alive"; cf. AcPetVerc 2:7; 11:19. But for the ms reading Turner conjectures *constituti*, "a regular Latin equivalent in this sort of Latin for οἱ ὄντες ('those who are') in Greek."

45

1

THE ACT OF PETER
(Berlin Coptic Codex: BG 8502,4, 128-141,7)

1 On the first day of the week, the Lord's day, a crowd gathered. ²They brought many sick people to Peter so that he would heal them.ᵃ

³Then someone in the crowd became bold and said to Peter, "Look, Peter, in our presence you have made many of the blind see; you have made the deaf hear; you have made the lame walk; and you have helped the weak and have given them strength. ⁴So, in the case of your virgin daughter, who has grown to be beautiful and has faith in the name of God, why didn't you help her? ⁵See, her one side is wholly paralyzed, and she lies there in that corner disabled. ⁶We see those you have healed, but your own daughter you have neglected."

⁷Peter laughed and said to him, "My son, it's evident to God himself why her body is not well. ⁸Know, then, that God has not been weak or unable to give his gift to my daughter! ⁹Now, so that your soul may be persuaded and those who are here may have greater faith ..."

1:2 ᵃCf. APeVer 29:1; Ac 5:16–17
1:7 ᵃ» APeVer 6:13

Title: • *The Act of Peter:* The title occurs both at the beginning of the document and as a colophon.
1:1 • *the first day of the week:* ⲣ̅ⲙ̅ ⲡⲟⲩⲁ ⲇⲉ [ⲙ̅]ⲡⲥⲁⲃⲃⲁⲧⲟⲛ = τῇ μίᾳ τῶν σαββάτων (Mark 16:2; Luke 24:1; John 20:1, 19; Acts 20:7); also Matt 28:1 εἰς μίαν σαββάτων; Mark 16:9 πρώτῃ σαββάτου (cf. 1 Cor 16:2 κατὰ μίαν σαββάτου, v.l. σαββάτων). See also AcPetVerc 7:1.
• *the Lord's Day* (ⲧⲕⲩⲣⲓⲁⲕⲏ) = (ἡ) κυριακή (sc. ἡμέρα), that is, Sunday; see already Rev 1:10; also AcPetVerc 29:4; AcPetMart 1(30):1; AcAndPas 13:2; AcJohn 106:2; AcPaul 7.4:6; AcThom 29:4; 31:9.
1:7 • *Peter laughed* (ⲁⲡⲉⲧⲣⲟⲥ] ⲇⲉ ⲥⲱⲃⲉ): ⲥⲱⲃⲉ means principally "to laugh, play"; see the Greek verbs cited in Crum, s.v. (pp. 320b–21a: γαλᾶν, παίζειν [and compounds], and especially μειδιᾶν); also in AcPetMart 2(30):12; 2(31):5; and further refs. at AcPaulThec 4:1. For "smiling," see note on AcPetVerc 6:13.
• *it's evident ... why,* or perhaps, "God alone knows why"; cf. AcPetVerc 2:22.

1:16 ªCf. ATh 41:1

[10]Then he looked at his daughter and said to her, "Rise from your place! [11]Let no one give you a hand except Jesus himself, and walk in front of all of these being healthy, and come to me!"

[12]She rose up and came to him, and the crowd rejoiced because of what had happened.

[13]Peter said to them, "Look, your hearts have been persuaded that God is not powerless concerning anything that we ask of him." [14]Then they rejoiced all the more and praised God.

[15]Peter <then> said to his daughter, "Go to your place, sit down, and return to your infirmity, for this is beneficial for you and for me." [16]The girl went back again, sat down in her place, and became again as she was before.ª

[17]The whole crowd wept and begged Peter to make her healthy. [18]So Peter said to them, "As the Lord lives, this is beneficial for her and for me! [19]For on the day she was born to me, I had a vision, and the Lord said to me, 'Peter, today a great trial has been born to you, for this one will harm many souls if her body remains healthy.' [20]<At the time,> I thought the vision was mocking me; but as soon as the girl got to be ten years old, many were scandalized by her. [21]Ptolemy, in particular, a man rich in property who had seen the girl bathing with her mother—he sent for her to take her for his wife. [22]And when her mother could not be persuaded, he <continued to> send for her many times; he couldn't wait.

(One leaf [i.e., two pages] is missing.)

1:11 • *give you a hand:* The Coptic idiom normally means "to help"; here it is translated literally so as to facilitate the identification of the same idea elsewhere in the *Acts of Peter*, e.g., in AcPetVerc 20:2; see also Mark 1:31 (= Matt 8:15; but cf. Luke 4:39); 5:41 (= Matt 9:25; Luke 8:54); 8:23 (no parallel Synoptic incident); 9:27 (not in the other Synoptic accounts); Acts 3:7; 9:41; Gal 2:9.

1:18 • *as the Lord lives* (ϥⲟⲛϩ ⲛ̄ϭⲓ ⲡⲭ̄ⲥ̄): A formula common in the historical and prophetic books of the OT (ⲙⲧ חי־יהוה ; ʟxx ζῇ κύριος).

1:21 • *to take her for his wife:* Marriage legislation passed under Augustus set the minimum age of marriage for girls at twelve years but allowed for a betrothed girl to be brought into her future husband's household at ten years of age. The consent of the girl and the girl's family was required in either case. These laws applied only to Roman citizens, but they give some idea of the general expectations of marriage at the time. Ptolemy's initial proposal is not outrageous; his subsequent actions are.

1:22 • *he couldn't wait,* or possibly "couldn't stop."

1:22 *couldn't wait:* In the missing portion of text, it seems clear that Ptolemy takes the girl to his house. Augustine (*C. Adim.* 17.5) and AcPhil 142 both indicate that Peter's daughter becomes paralyzed as a result of her father's prayer. Molinari suggests that Ptolemy's action in the missing pages should be interpreted as an act of "abduction marriage" in the Roman tradition (2005: 175–76). Abduction marriage left the "bride" in a compromised position, no matter what the outcome. Parrott (Brashler and Parrott, 1979: 484) argues that the presumed abduction is to be understood in light of Deut 22:28–29 ("If a man meets a virgin who is not betrothed, . . ."); but this seems less likely.

2:7 ᵃCf. APeVer
4:17; 13:10; APeMar
4(33):1; APaTh 7:1;
1Th 4:4

2:11 ᵃCf. APeVer
2:25; 8:28

2:13 ᵃCf. Ac 12:6–9

2:14 ᵃCf. Jn 4:25

2 " . . .] Ptolemy's <men brought> the girl. ²They put her down in front of the door of the house and went away.

³"When her mother and I realized this, we went down and found the girl with the whole of one side of her body paralyzed and withered away—from her toes to her head. ⁴We took her <in>, praising the Lord who had saved his servant from defilement, pollution, and destruction. ⁵This is why the girl remains in the same condition to this day.

⁶"Now, it is fitting that you should know the deeds of Ptolemy. ⁷He was smitten in his heart, and he grieved night and dayᵃ over what had happened to him. ⁸<In fact,> because of the many tears he cried, he became blind. ⁹He decided to go and hang himself. ¹⁰But look what happened: in the ninth hour of that day, when he was alone in his bedroom, <he> saw a great light that illuminated the whole house; ¹¹and he heard a voice saying to him, 'Ptolemy, God has not given his vesselsᵃ for corruption and pollution. ¹²Rather, since you believed in me, you cannot defile my virgin, whom you should know as a sister, because I have become one Spirit to both of you. ¹³Get up and go quicklyᵃ to Peter's—that is, to the apostle's—house, and you will see my glory. ¹⁴He will explain everythingᵃ to you.'

¹⁵"Ptolemy didn't delay. He commanded his men to show him the way and to bring him to me.

¹⁶"When he had come to me, he told me everything that had happened to him in the power of Jesus Christ our Lord. ¹⁷Then he saw <again> with the eyes of his flesh and the eyes of his soul, and many placed their hope in Christ. ¹⁸He did good things for them and gave them the gift of God. ¹⁹Later, Ptolemy died, and leaving <this> life he went to his Lord. ²⁰But when he <had made> his will, he assigned a piece of land to the name of my daughter, since it was

2:3 • *from her toes to her head,* literally, "from her toenails to her head." Cf. AcPetVerc 2:8, where Rufina suffers paralysis from her head to her toenails.
2:10 • *the ninth hour,* that is, the hour of prayer; see Acts 3:1; 10:30; AcPetVerc 17:11, 23, 44; 21:1.
2:17 • *the eyes of his flesh and the eyes of his soul:* This contrast is a commonplace in Neoplatonic philosophy. In Christian tradition see, e.g., *1 Clem.* 19:3 τοῖς ὄμμασιν τῆς ψυχῆς ("the eyes of the soul"); Justin *Dial.* 134.5 "the eyes of your soul are excessively weak"; Clement of Alexandria *Paed.* 2.9 "understanding is the eye of the soul" (cf. *Strom.* 7.16 "if one is curable ... let him lend the ears of the soul"); Origen *C. Cels.* 2.54; 7.39; Methodius *Symp.* 11.3; Augustine *Conf.* 7.10; AcPetVerc 21:2–4; AcPetMart 10(39):3 ("ears of the flesh"); AcAndPas 57:9; AcJohn 113:4; AcThom 28:2; 53:6; 65:6 "eyes of the mind (τῆς ἐννοίας)"; 166:2 "eyes of understanding (τῆς διανοίας)" (v.l. τῆς καρδίας "of the heart," as in Eph 1:18; *1 Clem.* 36:2; 59:3; *Mart. Pol.* 2:3); 143:7 (implicit contrast with "bodily eyes").

because of her he had come to faith in God and had been saved. ²¹Being entrusted with it, I saw to its administration most carefully: ²²I sold the land and, as God himself knows, neither I nor my daughter kept back any of the price of the land, but I gave all the money to the poor. ²³Know then, O servant of Christ Jesus, that God provides for those who are his, and he prepares what is good for each one. ²⁴And meanwhile we suppose that God has forgotten us! ²⁵So now, brothers and sisters, let us lament, be watchful, and pray! God's goodness will look down on us as we wait for it."

²⁶Peter also taught other things in the presence of them all, praising the name of the Lord, Christ. ²⁷He gave them all some of the bread; and when he had distributed it, he stood up and went home.

THE ACT OF PETER

2:22 • *as God himself knows,* or possibly "as God alone knows"; cf. AcPetBG 1:7.
    • *kept back any of the price:* The narrative seems to reflect the influence of the Ananias and Sapphira episode in Acts 5:1–11.
2:27 • *He gave them all …:* In AcPetVerc 5:30–31, Peter gives Theon bread after his baptism. In AcPetVerc 2:1, Paul celebrates the eucharist with bread and water.

2:22 *neither I nor my daughter:* Here the ms repeats the phrase "I sold the land."

2

THE ACTS OF PETER
THE APOSTLE
(Actus Vercellenses)

1 While Paul stayed in Rome and confirmed many in the faith, it happened that a woman named Candida heard Paul, paid attention to his preaching, and believed. [2]She was the wife of Quartus,[a] who was in charge of the guards. [3]She instructed her husband as well, and he believed; indeed, Quartus gave Paul permission to go wherever he wished away from the city. [4]Paul said to him, "If it is God's will <that I go here or there>, he will reveal it to me."[a]

[5]After he fasted for three days and asked the Lord what was fitting, Paul saw a vision of the Lord saying to him, [6]"Paul, get up and become in your body a physician to those who live in Spain!"

[7]Paul reported to the brothers and sisters what God had ordered <him to do>, and without hesitation he was ready to set out from the city. [8]But just when he was about to leave, there was great weeping throughout the whole fellowship, because they believed they would not see Paul again[a] —they tore their garments <at the news>. [9]They also had in mind that Paul had frequently been in dispute with the teachers of the Jews, and that he had refuted <them, saying>, [10]"Surely Christ, the one on whom your fathers laid their hands, destroyed their Sabbath along with <their> fasts, <their> feasts, and circumcision. [11]Likewise, he destroyed <all> human teaching and other traditions."[a]

[12]Now the brothers and sisters mourned <and urged> Paul by the return of our Lord Jesus Christ to be absent for no more than

1:2 [a]Cf. Rm 16:23

1:4 [a]Cf. APeMar 6 (35):2–3

1:8 [a]Cf. Ac 20:38

1:11 [a]Cf. Col 2:8–23

• *The Acts of Peter the Apostle:* This is the title conjectured by Schmidt by analogy with others of the apocryphal acts. In the Lipsius-Bonnet edition (*Aaa* 1. 45–103) this portion of the AcPet is entitled *Actus Petri cum Simone* ("The Acts of Peter and [*or:* with] Simon"). See the note on AcPetMart 12(41):6.
1:2 • *in charge of the guards:* Poupon (1997: 1054) understands this obscure passage to refer to a form of house arrest.

1:3 *gave Paul permission (permisit):* Turner's conjecture for *permansit* ("persisted, remained"); otherwise possibly *persuasit*, "persuaded" (so Lipsius). **1:6** *in your body (corpori tuo):* This is what the ms reads; the phrase can also mean "while you are still alive"; cf. AcPetVerc 2:7; 11:19. But for the ms reading Turner conjectures *constituti*, "a regular Latin equivalent in this sort of Latin for οἱ ὄντες ('those who are') in Greek."

1:15 [a]Cf. Ac 9:15–16

2:1 [a]» APeBG 2:27

2:3 [a]Cf. APeVer 6:13; Ac 6:3, 5; 7:55; 11:24; 13:52; Eph 5:18

2:4 [a]Cf. 1Cor 11:27–28; ATh 51:2

2:5 [a]Cf. Ac 14:15; 1Th 1:9; 1Jn 5:20; APeVer 2:13; 9:10; 12:16; 17:25; 23;17; 28:23

[b]Cf. Rm 8:27

2:6 [a]Cf. 1Jn 1:9

2:7 [a]» APeVer 1:6

[b]Cf. Mt 8:12; 13:42; 22:13; 25:30

2:8 [a]Cf. APeBG 2:3

2:10 [a]Cf. APeVer 2:11, 13; 17:18; AcPeMar 9:10

a year, saying, "We know your care concerning your brothers and sisters. [13]Don't forget us when you arrive there and start to abandon us like children without a mother!"

[14]After they had entreated him with tears for a long time, there came a sound from heaven and a loud voice saying, "Paul, the servant of God, is chosen for lifetime service. [15]By the hand of Nero, an impious and evil man, he will be killed before your eyes."[a] [16]Again, great awe came over the brothers and sisters because of the voice that had come from heaven, and many were further confirmed.

2 They brought Paul bread and water for the sacrifice, so that, after the prayers, he should distribute <them> to each one. [2]Among <those present> there happened to be a woman named Rufina, who also wanted to receive the eucharist from the Paul's hands. [3]As she came near, Paul, who was filled with the spirit of God,[a] said, "Rufina, you are not approaching the altar of God as one who is worthy. [4]You have got up from being beside not your husband, but an adulterer —yet <still> you try to receive God's eucharist.[a] [5]Look out! Satan will weigh in on your heart, and cast you down before the eyes of all who believe in the Lord, so that when they see and believe, they will know they have believed in the living God,[a] the one who scrutinizes hearts.[b] [6]<Now,> if you repent of your deed, the one who is able to blot out your sin and to free you from this sin is faithful.[a] [7]<But> if you don't repent while you are still in your body, the devastating fire and the outer darkness shall receive you for all the ages."[a]

[8]At that instant Rufina fell, paralyzed on her left side from head to toe.[a] [9]She <even> lost her power of speech, because her tongue was tied.

[10]When those who believed in faith and the neophytes saw this, they beat their breasts, they remembered their previous sins,[a] and

---

2:2 • *Rufina*: Cf. 1 Cor 11:29; this story is mentioned in Ps.-Titus 3.26–33.

2:4 • *adulterer*: *moechus* normally means "adulterer." Poupon (1997: 1056 n. B) translates "lover" ("amant"), and suggests that Rufina should be understood as a concubine. Vouaux (1922: 235 n. 6) notes that this scene shows that abstinence within marriage is not required for participation in the eucharist.

2:10 • *believed in faith* (*credentes in fidem*), or "believed in *the* faith," if *fides* (πίστις) has here technical force, its having by the early second century become "a historical term, so to speak, for becoming or being Christian or also for Christianity in the sense of the content of its belief" (Bultmann, 1951–55: 2. 211; hence BAGD, s.v. πίστις 3. "That which is believed, *body of faith* or *belief, doctrine*"); see Jude 3, 20; IEph 16:2.

 • *the neophytes* (*neofiti*): Also in AcPetVerc 7:20; in the NT only at 1 Tim 3:6 (νεόφυτος, literally, "newly planted"; Vulg. *neophytus*)—the bishop is not to be "a recent convert"; cf. 1 Cor 3:6, 10–11. Similarly AcPetVerc 36:5 "[the Lord] will ... cause you, whom he planted, to grow in him, so that you too can plant others"; also AcAndMatt 32:6; AcAndPas 12:8; further refs. in LPGL, s.v. (p. 905a).

they lamented, saying, [11]"We do not know if God will forgive us the sins which we committed previously."[a]

[12]So Paul asked for silence:[a] "Brothers and sisters," he said, "you who are now beginning to believe in Christ: [13]If you do not persist in your previous works,[a] in the tradition of your fathers, and if you abstain from all deceit, anger, cruelty, adultery, and impurity, and from pride, jealousy, haughtiness, and enmity, then Jesus, the living God,[b] will forgive what you did in ignorance.[c] [14]So, servants of God, let each one of you arm for yourselves your inner person, <so that you will have> peace, equanimity, gentleness, faith, charity, knowledge, wisdom, mutual love, hospitality, mercy, abstinence, chastity, goodness, and justice. [15]Then you will have the firstborn of all creatures as your guide for eternity,[a] along with virtue, in peace, with our Lord."

[16]When they heard this from Paul, they asked him to pray for them. [17]So Paul raised his voice and said, "Eternal God, God of Heaven, God of ineffable divinity, who has confirmed all things by your word,[a] who has covered the whole world with the fast bonds of your grace, [18]Father of your holy Son, Jesus Christ, we pray to you, in turn, by your son Jesus Christ, strengthen our souls, which previously were unbelieving but now are faithful! [19]I was once a blasphemer, but now I am blasphemed;[a] I was once a persecutor, but now I suffer persecution from others. [20]Once an enemy of Christ,[a] now I pray to be a friend; I trust in his promise and his mercy. [21]I think that I am faithful, and that I have received forgiveness for my former offenses.[a] [22]Therefore, I urge you, too, brothers and sisters, to have faith in the Lord, Father omnipotent, and to have every hope in our Lord Jesus Christ, his Son. [23]If you believe in him, no one will be able to remove you from his promise. [24]In the same way, bend your knees[a] and commend me to the Lord, as I am about to set out toward another nation, so that his grace may go before me and he may arrange my departure well. [25]Then he will be able to take up his holy vessels and his faithful ones, and they will be well founded, giving thanks that I preached the word of the Lord."

[26]The brothers and sisters, however, cried and for Paul's sake pleaded with the Lord for a long time, saying, [27]"Lord Jesus Christ,

2:11 [a]» APeVer 2:10

2:12 [a]Cf. Ac 15:12; 21:40

2:13 [a]» APeVer 2:10

[b]» APeVer 2:5

[c]Cf. Ac 3:17; 17:30; Eph 4:18; 1Pt 1:14

2:15 [a]Cf. Col 1:15

2:17 [a]Cf. Ps 33:6

2:19 [a]Cf. 1Cor 10:30

2:20 [a]Cf. APeVer 12:11; AJn 84:13

2:21 [a]Cf. APeVer 2:10; 1Tm 1:12–14

2:24 [a]Cf. APeVer 3:1; 18:5; APaTh 5:1; 24:1; APa 8.2:2

2:18 • we pray … in turn (invicem), or "we pray … together"; see also AcPetVerc 3:9.

2:14 <so that you will have> peace: The phrase is added from *Vit. Aberc.* f. 133.

3:1 ª» APeVer 2:24
3:4 ªCf. Rm 16:11
4:2 ªCf. Ac 8:10

be with Paul and return him to us unharmed, for we know our infirmity, which is still in us!"

3 A great crowd of women, kneeling[a] and praying, made their petitions to blessed Paul, kissed his feet, and accompanied him to the port— [2]along with Dionysius and Balbus from Asia, who were Roman knights and distinguished men. [3]A senator named Demetrius, who held close to Paul's right side, said, "Paul, if I were not a magistrate, I would choose to flee the city in order not to part from you." [4]Cleobis, Iphitis, and Lysimachus, who belonged to the household of Caesar, and two matrons, Berenice and Philostrata, together with the presbyter Narcissus,[a] <spoke> in the same way as they accompanied him to the port.

[5]Because a storm threatened at sea, he sent the brothers and sisters back to Rome, so that whoever wished might come down and listen to Paul until he sailed. [6]In response, the brothers and sisters went up into the city. [7]When they brought the message to the brothers and sisters who had remained in the city, the word spread rapidly. [8]<So> they came down to the port—some riding on animals, some by foot, others by way of the Tiber. [9]For three days, and until the fifth hour of the fourth day, they were confirmed in their faith as they prayed in turn with Paul, and made offerings. [10]They put whatever was necessary in the ship and gave him two faithful young men who would sail with him. [11]They bade him farewell in the Lord, and themselves returned to Rome.

4 After a few days there was a great commotion in the church, when some said that they had seen marvels done by a man named Simon, and that he was in Aricia. [2]They added, "He says that he is the Great Power of God[a] and does nothing without God. Can this be the Christ? [3]However, we have faith in the one whom Paul preached to us, since we have seen the dead raised through him and others freed from various infirmities. [4]Yet we understand that this fellow is looking for contests, so there has been no small disturbance. [5]Perhaps he will enter Rome soon—<as recently as> yesterday he was urged on with great acclamations, when they said to him, [6]"You are God in Italy! You are Savior of the Romans! Hasten quickly to

3:4 • *the household of Caesar* would include numerous slaves and freedmen who might carry out administrative duties of various sorts. The expression is found in the NT at Phil 4:22.
3:9 • *prayed in turn* (*invicem*), or "prayed together"; see note on AcPetVerc 2:18.
4:2 • *Can this be the Christ? Numquid ipse est Christus?* as in John 4:29 Vulg. (Greek μήτι οὗτός ἐστιν ὁ Χριστός;).

Rome!' [7]He spoke to the people simply, saying, 'Tomorrow you will see me, at about the seventh hour, flying above the gate of the city in the same state in which you now see me speaking with you.' [8]So, brothers and sisters, if you want to see, let's go and watch carefully what happens."

[9]So they all ran together, and came to the gate. It was the seventh hour and, yes, suddenly <a cloud of> dust was visible in the sky at a distance—like shining smoke with fiery projections. [10]After it arrived at the gate it suddenly disappeared. [11]Then he appeared in the midst[a] of the crowd: they all honored him and recognized him as the one who had appeared to them the previous day. [12]The brothers and sisters were scandalized among themselves more than a little, especially because Paul was not in Rome. [13]Neither was Timothy nor Barnabas present, for they had been sent to Macedonia by Paul.[a] [14]So there was no one to strengthen them. They were, moreover, <only> recently instructed.

[15]Simon exalted himself greatly by the things he did. In their daily conversations some of them called Paul a magician; others, a deceiver. [16]Thus of the great multitude established in faith all were lost except Narcissus, the presbyter, two women in the Bithynian hospice, and four who were no longer able to leave their homes. [17]Being confined there, they were free for prayers, night and day.[a] [18]They asked the Lord to bring Paul back quickly, or someone else who could visit his servants, since the devil had destroyed them by his wickedness.

5 While they mourned and fasted, God was already preparing Peter in Jerusalem for what was to come. [2]When the twelve years which the Lord had prescribed for him were fulfilled, Christ showed him a vision like this: [3]He said to him, "Peter, the one whom you cast out of Judea, Simon, whom you proved to be a magician, has again gained a foothold ahead of you at Rome. [4]In brief, you should know that Satan, whose power Simon proves himself to be, has destroyed all those who had faith in me by means of his cunning

4:11 [a]Cf. APeVer 9:11, 12; 23:3; 28:2, 15

4:13 [a]Cf. Ac 19:22; Phil 2:19–20

4:17 [a]»APeBG 2:7

4:9 • *like shining smoke with fiery projections:* Herodotus (*Hist.* 8.65) reports a similar epiphany in connection with the battle of Salamis.

5:2 • *twelve years:* The tradition that the apostles were told to remain in Jerusalem for twelve years is also found in the *Kerygma Petrou* (*apud* Clement of Alexandria *Strom.* 6.5.43) and in the anti-Montanist writings of Apollonius as quoted in Eusebius *Hist. eccl.* 5.18.14.

5:3 • *you proved to be a magician:* The author betrays a knowledge of the NT book of Acts, or of some noncanonical tradition to the same effect.

• *ahead of you:* The "you" is plural, signifying Peter and the Christian movement generally.

5:7 ªCf. APeVer 6:31

and activities. [5]Don't delay! Set out tomorrow! You will find a ship, ready there, that is sailing to Italy. [6]In a few days I shall show you my grace, which knows no grudging."

[7]Peter, admonished by this vision, reported it to the brothers and sisters without delay, saying, "I must go up to Rome to defeat the foe and enemy of our Lord[a] and of our brothers and sisters." [8]He went down to Caesarea, and immediately, without bringing any provisions on board, he embarked on a ship that already had its gangway drawn up. [9]The captain, named Theon, looked at Peter and said, "Whatever we have is yours, for what thanks would we deserve, if we took on a man like ourselves who is in uncertain circumstances and did not share all that we have with you. [10]Only let us have a successful voyage." [11]Peter thanked him for his offer, but fasted during the voyage, mourning in his spirit. [12]Yet he comforted himself with the fact that God considered him a worthy servant in his ministry.

[13]After a few days the captain arose at his meal time and asked Peter to eat with him. [14]He said, "Whoever you may be, whether god or human, I scarcely know you; but, as I judge, I consider you a servant of God. [15]During the night, while the ship was under my watch, I fell asleep, and I had a vision. [16]A human voice was speaking to me from heaven, 'Theon! Theon!' [17]Twice it called me by name and said to me, 'Of all those sailing with you, let Peter be most honored by you. [18]Because of him, you and the others will be safe, without any injury, by way of an inspired voyage.' "

[19]Since Peter thought that God wished to reveal his providence at sea to those who were in the ship, he began then to explain to Theon the mighty acts of God: [20]how the Lord had chosen him among the apostles, and the reason he was sailing to Italy. [21]Thus, daily, he shared with him the preaching of God. [22]He observed him

---

5:16 • *Theon! Theon!* The double call of a human's name has numerous biblical precedents, e.g., in Luke 10:41; Acts 9:4; 22:7; 26:14.

5:18 • *inspired voyage:* The vision refers to the rapid arrival of the ship thanks to a divinely ordered wind. The force of the saying is weakened by such proposed emendations as "unexpected course" (Usener) and "unexpected finish" (Lipsius). Turner's emendation, "uninjured from an <unexpected event>" has the voice predict a danger that does not transpire. If the *Acts of Paul* is dependent on the *Acts of Peter*, it would appear that in AcPaul [*P. Hamb.* 7] this scene is conflated with AcPetMart 6(35), where Peter meets Christ at the gates of Rome.

5:19 • *the mighty acts of God: magnalia dei,* as in Acts 2:11 Vulg. for τὰ μεγαλεῖα τοῦ θεοῦ, the sole NT occurrence of the phrase; see also AcPetVerc 6:16 ("his great and marvelous deeds"); 17:9; 28:20; AcAndMatt 10:2; AcJohn 37:2; AcPaulThec 1:3 τὰ μεγαλεῖα τοῦ χριστοῦ ("the great deeds *of Christ*"); 18:2; AcPaul 6:1. The phrase is apparently absent from the *Acts of Thomas.*

and recognized by his behavior that he was in accord with the faith and a worthy servant. [23]So, when a calm settled on the ship in the Adriatic, Theon pointed out the calm to Peter and said to him, [24]"If you are willing to consider me worthy to be one you baptize with the sign of the Lord, you have an opportunity"—for all in the ship were in a drunken stupor. [25]Peter climbed down by a line, and baptized Theon in the name of the Father, Son, and Holy Spirit.[a] [26]As he came up out of the water rejoicing greatly, Peter was cheered because he [God] had considered Theon worthy of his name.

[27]Then, in the spot where Theon was baptized, a youth with radiant beauty[a] appeared and said to them, "Peace be with you!" [28]Peter and Theon went up and entered the cabin immediately. [29]Because the Lord had made him worthy of his holy ministry and because the youth had appeared to them, saying, "Peace be with you," [30]Peter took bread and gave thanks to the Lord: "Best and only Holy One, you who indeed appeared to us, God, Jesus Christ, in your name he was just now <washed> and marked with your holy sign. [31]Therefore, in your name I now give him your eucharist, so that he will be your perfect servant without fault forever."[a]

[32]Now as they feasted and rejoiced in the Lord, a breeze came up which was not violent but moderate and blowing across the stern. [33]It did not cease for six full days[a] and nights—until they had arrived at Puteoli.

6 When they had landed at Puteoli, Theon left the ship and went to the lodging house where he usually stayed in order to prepare it to receive Peter. [2]Ariston, the man with whom he stayed, feared the Lord always, and Theon entrusted himself to him because of the name. [3]When Theon arrived at his lodging and saw Ariston, he said to him, [4]"The God who has considered you worthy to serve him has also given me his gift by the hands of his holy servant Peter, who sailed with me from Judea because he was commanded to come to Italy by our Lord."

5:30 *washed* (*lotus*), is corrected from *locutus* ("spoken") (so Lipsius).

5:26 • *his name:* Theon's name suggests "godly" character (θεός); but the act of taking on the name "Christian" may also be in view, as the succeeding events suggest.
5:27 • *Peace be with you! Pax vobis,* as in John 20:19, 21, 26 Vulg. (Greek εἰρήνη ὑμῖν); cf. AcAndMatt 3:5; 4:8; AcThom 27:2.

5:25 [a]Cf. Mt 28:19; ATh 27:10
5:27 [a]Cf. AJn 87:2; APa 7.4:8; ATh 27:11
5:31 [a]» APeBG 2:27
5:33 [a]» APaTh 23:7

6:12 ᵃ» APeVer 2:5
6:13 ᵃ» APeVer 2:3
6:15 ᵃCf. Jn 17:12

⁵When Ariston heard this, he threw himself on Theon's neck. Embracing him <in this way>, he asked Theon to lead him to the ship and show Peter to him. ⁶Ariston explained that since Paul had departed for Spain, there was no one in the fellowship with whom he could refresh himself. ⁷Moreover, a Jew named Simon had <newly> burst in on the city: ⁸"With his magic spell and his wickedness," <Ariston said,> "he has destroyed the whole fellowship on all sides; that's why I fled from Rome, hoping that Peter would come. ⁹Paul had spoken of him, and I myself have seen many things in a vision. ¹⁰Now, therefore, I trust in my Lord since he is rebuilding his ministry and will remove every seduction from his servants. ¹¹Our Lord Jesus Christ, who is able to restore our minds, is indeed faithful."

¹²When Theon heard this from the weeping Ariston, his spirit grew stronger and he was further confirmed because he knew that he had believed in the living God.ᵃ ¹³When they arrived at the ship together and Peter saw them, he smiled, since he was filled with the Spirit.ᵃ ¹⁴So Ariston fell to his face at Peter's feet and said, "Brother and lord, you who impart the holy mysteries and show the upright way which is in the Lord Jesus Christ, our God, who in turn shows us his own coming in you— ¹⁵because of Satan's activities we have lost all those whom Paul gave us.ᵃ ¹⁶But now I trust in the Lord, who sent you as his messenger and commanded you to come to us because he has considered us worthy to see his great and marvelous deeds

---

6:7 • *a Jew named Simon (Judaeum quendam ... nomine Simonem):* Simon is identified as a Jew, rather than as a Samaritan; see also AcPetVerc 22:17. Likewise, his confrontation with the apostles is placed in Jerusalem, or more generally in Judea, rather than in Samaria; see AcPetVerc 5:3; 9:4; 17:1–2, 11, 53, 56; 23:11, 14.
6:12 • *he had believed:* The subject is presumably Ariston, but this is not certain.
6:13 • *he smiled (subrisit):* Similarly, of "someone in the crowd" (*quendam in turba*) in AcPetVerc 11:2 (*subridentem*); 11:3; of Jesus (in Peter's vision) in 16:1 (*subridentem*). As elsewhere in the apocryphal acts, except the *Acts of Thomas*, smiling (μειδιᾶν; or, less often, laughing, γελᾶν) denotes special insight or foreknowledge. See AcAndGE 16:3; AcAndPas 3:4; 55(5):2; AcJohn 73:1; AcPaulThec 4:1 "Paul smiled" (ἐμειδίασεν); AcPaul 7.3:8; 7.5:8; *Ep. apost.* 14:5 "Sarah laughed" (cf. Gen 18:12); Herm. *Vis.* 1.1:8 "[Rhoda] laughed (γελάσασα) and said to me"; PsClemRec 1.47:3; PsClemHom 2.50:1; *Ap. John* (NHC II,1) 22,12 "The savior smiled and said"; 26.25–26 "And he smiled and said to me"; *Soph. Jes. Chr.* (NHC III,4) 91,22–92,3 "The Savior laughed." The motif goes back to Homer, e.g., *Od.* 16.476 (μείδησαν); 20.301 (μείδησεν); for laughter see, e.g., Euripides *Bacc.* 439 (γελᾶν); and the note on AcPetBG 1:7, above.
6:16 • *his great and marvelous deeds (magnalia et mirabilia sua):* See note on AcPetVerc 5:19.

6:14 *who in turn ... in you:* Turner emends to "who has openly shown us your coming."

<done> through you. [17]I beg you, therefore, hurry into the city—I left behind the brothers and sisters who have been scandalized, whom I saw falling into the devil's temptation. [18]I fled to this place, saying to them, 'Brothers and sisters, stand fast in the faith! [19]It is certain that within these two months the mercy of our Lord will bring you his servant.' [20]I had seen a vision—Paul <himself> saying to me, 'Ariston, flee from the city!' [21]When I heard this, I believed without delay and departed in the Lord. [22]Even though I bear an infirmity in my flesh,[a] I came here and stood every day at the shore asking the sailors, 'Did Peter sail with you?' [23]Now, that the grace of the Lord is overflowing; so I ask you, let's go up to the city without delay, so that the teaching of that most wicked man not grow stronger."

[24]As Ariston said this in tears, Peter gave him his hand and lifted him from the ground. [25]Peter also sighed, and said to him—himself in tears, "He who tempts the whole world by means of his angels has, <it's true,> a foothold ahead of us; [26]but the one who has the power to remove his servants from all temptation will extinguish his seductions and place him beneath the feet of those who have faith in Christ, whom we preach."[a]

[27]As they went in the gate, Theon questioned Peter, saying, "You didn't take refreshment any of the days on the ship during the long voyage. [28]<So> are you going to set out now on such a rough road, straight from the ship? [29]Stay, rather, and refresh yourself, and you will set out <refreshed,> as you should be. [30]The road from here to Rome is paved with stone, and I fear that you will suffer from the shaking."

[31]Peter replied, "If it should so happen to me that I, along with the enemy of our Lord,[a] be hung with a millstone and cast into the deep— [32]just as my Lord said to us, 'If one causes any of the brothers or sisters to stumble ...'—[33]then it would be <a matter> not of the millstone only, but of what is worse: that the opponent of this persecutor of his servants would reach his end far from those who believe in the Lord, Jesus Christ."

6:22 [a]Cf. Gal 4:12
6:26 [a]Cf. Rm 16:20
6:31 [a]Cf. APeVer 5:7

6:18 • *stand fast in the faith! state in fide*, as in 1 Cor 16:13 Vulg. (Greek στήκετε ἐν τῇ πίστει).
6:32 • *If one causes ... to stumble (si quis de fratribus scandalizasset)*: Cf. Matt 18:6; Mark 9:42; Luke 17:2.

6:33 *that the opponent of ... Jesus Christ:* The passage is corrupt, but the sense seems to be that if Peter fails to stop the influence of Simon immediately, then his own fate will be no better that Simon's; and the consequence for the faithful in Rome will likewise be disastrous.

7:4 [a]Cf. AcPeBG 1:1

7:5 [a]Cf. Jn 3:16

[b]Cf. ATh 143:6

7:8 [a]Cf. Ac 3:17;
1Cor 2:8

7:10 [a]Cf. Ac 1:21

7:11 [a]Cf. Mt 26:34–
35; Mk 14:30–31; Lk
22:34

7:12 [a]Cf. Ps 22:16

[34]Theon was not able to persuade him by any argument to remain there for even one day. [35]Theon, for his part, entrusted everything in the ship to be sold for its proper value. [36]He also followed Peter to Rome, where Ariston brought him into the house of Narcissus the presbyter.

7 The report flew around the city to the scattered brothers and sisters that Peter, the disciple of the Lord, had come on account of Simon— [2]so as to unmask him as a seducer and persecutor of good people. [3]The whole multitude ran together to see the Lord's apostle being established in Christ.

[4]On the first day of the week,[a] when a crowd gathered to see Peter, he began to speak in his loudest voice: [5]"You here who hope in Christ, you who have briefly suffered temptation, learn the reason that God sent his son into the world,[a] or the reason he brought him forth by the Virgin Mary.[b] [6]Wasn't it to produce some sort of grace or providence, since he wished <to eliminate> every obstacle, all ignorance, and every activity of the devil, [7]and to annul the principles and powers by which that one used to have his way, before our God shone forth in the world?

[8]"Because they fell into death through many and varied infirmities on account of ignorance,[a] the omnipotent God was moved by compassion and sent his son into the world. [9]I was with him—I even walked on water. [10]I myself remain as a witness to him: When he was active in the world through the signs and wonders which he did, I was present.[a]

[11]"I do confess, dearest brothers and sisters, that I denied our Lord Jesus Christ not only once but three times[a]— [12]there were wicked 'dogs surrounding me,'[a] just as the Lord's prophet <had said>. [13]But the Lord didn't blame me; instead, he turned towards

---

6:34 • *for even one day:* There is perhaps a deliberate contrast here with the "seven days" of Acts 28:14.

7:7 • *principles and powers* (*initia et vires*): The Greek antecedent, according to Vouaux (1922: 272 n. 3), will have been ἀρχαὶ καὶ δυνάμεις, as in AcJohn 98:9; cf. 1 Cor 15:24; Eph 1:21; 6:12; Col 2:10, 15.

• *have his way:* This phrase is supplied from *Vit. Aberc.* f. 136.

7:9 • *I even walked on water:* This incident, which is mentioned again in AcPetVerc 10:13, shows familiarity with the Gospel of Matthew (here, 14:28–32).

7:13 • *he turned towards me:* This detail is the clearest evidence of the author's knowledge of the Gospel of Luke (here, 22:61).

7:1 *that Peter, the disciple of the Lord, had come:* Turner "saying that Peter had come to Rome."

me. [14]He had compassion on the weakness of my flesh— [15]so that later I lamented bitterly and mourned that my faith had been so weak, because I had been deprived of sense by the devil and did not keep in mind the word of my Lord.

[16]Now, I say to you, brothers and sisters who have gathered in the name of Jesus Christ: the deceiver Satan aims his arrows at you as well,[a] to make you depart from the path. [17]Don't fail, brothers and sisters. Don't lose heart! But be strong, persevere, and don't doubt! [18]For if Satan caused me, whom the Lord held in highest honor, to fall, so that I denied the light of my hope— [19]if by subjecting me he persuaded me to flee, as though I had believed in a mere human[a]— [20]what are you, who are <mere> neophytes,[a] to think? [21]Do you think that he would not overthrow you, so as to make you enemies of the kingdom of God and cast you into perdition[a] by means of his newest deception? [22]<You surely know that> whoever he has dispossessed of the hope of our Lord Jesus Christ is a child of perdition for eternity. [23]Be converted, therefore, brothers and sisters, you who are chosen by God! [24]Be strong in the Lord omnipotent, the Father of our Lord Jesus Christ, whom no one has ever seen,[a] nor is anyone able to see, except those who have faith in him. [25]Therefore, understand where this temptation of yours has come from. [26]For I wish not only to persuade you with words that this one whom I preach is the Christ, but also to exhort you by means of deeds[a] and magnificent acts of power done through the faith that is in Christ Jesus. [27]And this is why: so that none of you will look for another beside the one who was despised and mocked by the Jews—this Nazarene who was crucified, dead, and raised on the third day."

8 When the brothers and sisters had repented, they asked Peter to overcome Simon, who said he was the Power of God. [2]He was staying in the house of Marcellus, a senator who was persuaded by Simon's spells. [3]"Believe us, brother Peter!" they said. "No one was

---

7:16 [a]Cf. Eph 6:16

7:19 [a]Cf. APeVer 14:11

7:20 [a]Cf. APeVer 2:10

7:21 [a]Cf. APeVer 12:5

7:24 [a]Cf. Ex 33:20; Jn 1:18; 1Jn 4:12

7:26 [a]Cf. APeVer 17:38

7:21 • *the kingdom of God* is mentioned only here and in 24:14. See also AcPetMart 9(38):8.

7:26 • *through the faith which is in Christ Jesus* (*per fidem quae est in Christo Jesu*): See also AcPetVerc 10:10; 17:24; 21:4. The phrase, with relative pronoun or equivalent, is reminiscent of 1 Tim 1:13 ἐν πίστει τῇ ἐν Χριστῷ Ἰησοῦ (Vulg. *in fide quae est in Christo Iesu*) and 2 Tim 1:13 ἐν πίστει καὶ ἀγάπῃ τῇ ἐν Χριστῷ Ἰησοῦ (*in fide et dilectione in Christo Iesu*); 3:15 διὰ πίστεως τῆς ἐν Χριστῷ Ἰησοῦ (*per fidem quae est in Christo Iesu*); and cf. Acts 26:18 (*per fidem quae est in me*). Similar, but without the relative pronoun or equivalent, is Col 1:4.

8:2 • *Marcellus, a senator:* Ficker (1903: 38) suggests that the historical prefect of Bithynia, Granius Marcellus, lies behind this character; see also AcThom 19:9.

8:5 ᵃCf. 3Jn 5–8

8:17 ᵃCf. Rm 2:5

ᵇCf. Mt 7:15; Ac 20:29

8:18 ᵃCf. APeMar
9(38):4–7

wiser among men than this Marcellus. All the widows who hoped
in Christ found refuge with him; all the orphans were fed by him.
⁴What is more, brother, all of the poor called Marcellus their patron— <in fact,> his house was said to belong to the foreigners and
the poor.ᵃ ⁵When the emperor said, 'I am holding you back from every office, lest you exploit the provinces and give to the Christians,'
⁶Marcellus answered: 'All my possessions are yours.' ⁷Caesar replied
<in turn>, 'They would be mine, if you had preserved them for me;
but now, because they are not mine, you give them to whomever
you wish—to anyone at all among the lowest people.'

⁸"Now with these things in mind, brother, we tell you that the
man's great mercy has been transformed into blasphemy. ⁹And the
fact is that if he had not been converted <by Simon>, we would
not have been removed from the holy faith in God, our Lord. ¹⁰But
now this Marcellus is furious <about his former life>. ¹¹He regrets
his benefactions—'So much property I expended for such a long a
time,' he says, 'vainly believing that I was paying for knowledge of
God.' ¹²So much so that if one of the foreigners approaches him at
the door of his house, he pounds him with his stick and has him attacked, saying, 'If only I had not paid out so much money for those
impostors!' ¹³He says many other blasphemous things as well. ¹⁴Yet
if the Lord's mercy and the goodness of his commands persist in
you at all, come for the correction of this man's error, who gave so
much in alms to the servants of God!"

¹⁵When Peter saw these things and was struck by great anguish,
he said:

¹⁶"O the varied artifices and temptations of the devil!
O the machinations and inventions of evils!
¹⁷He is building the greatest fire for himself on the day of wrath;ᵃ
He is the banisher of simple people, the rapacious wolf,ᵇ
the devourer and destroyer of eternal life!
¹⁸You ensnared the first human with desire, and, by your old
wickedness,
you bound him in bodily chains.ᵃ
¹⁹You are the altogether most bitter fruit of the tree of bitter-
ness,
which incites various desires.

8:9 • *from the holy faith* (*a sancta fide*): The closest NT antecedent to this (presumably) technical term is ἡ ἁγιωτάτη ὑμῶν πίστις ("your most holy faith") in Jude 20.
8:16–32 • *O the varied artifices…*: Cf. AcJohn 84:1–13; AcThom 44:1–6.

8:7 *give them to whomever you wish:* Turner conjec-
tures "they are not mine because you give them   away to whomever you wish."

²⁰You led Judas, my fellow disciple and fellow apostle,
>to act impiously and to betray our Lord Jesus Christ,
>who must exact punishment from you.

²¹You hardened the heart of Herod and inflamed Pharaoh,ᵃ
>and led him to contend against the holy servant of God,
>Moses.

²²You are responsible for the audacity of Caiaphas,ᵃ
>who unjustly handed our Lord Jesus Christ over to the crowd,
>and still you are shooting innocent soulsᵇ with your poisoned arrows.ᶜ

²³Wicked enemy of all, be accursed—set apart from the church
of the Son of the holy, omnipotent God!

²⁴Like a firebrand cast out of the hearth,
>you will be extinguished by the servants of our Lord Jesus Christ.

²⁵May your blackness be upon you and your offspring,
>a most evil seed!

²⁶May your wicked deeds be turned against you,
>and against you, your threats;

²⁷against you and your angels,
>your temptations—you who are the beginning of evil and the abyss of darkness!

²⁸May your own darkness be with you,
>and with your vessels, whom you possess.

²⁹Depart, then, from these who are to have faith in God!
>Depart from the servants of Christ, and from those who wish to fight for him!

³⁰Wear for yourself
>your tunic of darkness!

³¹Without reason you knock at other doors which belong not to you
>but to Christ Jesus who guards them.

³²You, therefore, rapacious wolf, wish to steal sheep who are not yours,
>but belong to Christ Jesus,
>who guards them diligently with the greatest care."

8:21 ᵃCf. Ex 7:3; Lk 23:11; ATh 32:10

8:22 ᵃCf. Mt 26:66–67; 27:2; Jn 18:35; Ac 4:27

ᵇCf. APeVer 15:12

ᶜCf. Eph 6:16

8:22 • *who unjustly . . .*: Vouaux (1922: 284–85 nn. 1, 6) notes the general rather than specific familiarity with (or at least allusion to) scriptural material.
8:30 • *tunic of darkness*: Cf. Herm. *Sim.* 9.9:5; 13.8; 15.3 (see Vouaux, 1922: 285 n. 7).
8:32 • *You therefore . . . greatest care*: This verse may include a polemical inversion of the Simonian use of the shepherd parable (cf. John 10:12) to explain Simon's mission in the world.

9:10 ᵃ» APeVer 2:5

9:11 ᵃ» APeVer 4:10

9:12 ᵃ» APeVer 4:10

10:3 ᵃCf. Mt 5:43–44;
Lk 6:27–28

9 While Peter said this with great anguish in his soul, many believers in the Lord were added. ²The brothers and sisters asked Peter to confront Simon so he would not be free to disturb the people any longer. ³Without delay, therefore, Peter left the assembly and went to Marcellus's house, where Simon was staying. Large crowds followed him.

⁴When he came to the door, he called the doorkeeper and said to him, "Go and tell Simon, 'Peter, because of whom you fled from Judea, is waiting for you at the door.' "

⁵The doorkeeper replied to Peter, "Whether you are Peter, I do not know, sir, but I have an order. ⁶He learned yesterday that you had entered the city, and he said to me, 'Whether by day or by night, at whatever hour he comes, say that I am not inside!' "

⁷Peter said to the youth, "You spoke well when you reported these things, since you were compelled by him." ⁸Peter turned to the people who were following him and said, "You are about to see a great and marvelous prodigy."

⁹Then Peter looked around and saw a large dog, tied with a great chain; he went over to it and set it free. ¹⁰Now freed, the dog took on a human voice and said to Peter, "What do you command me to do, servant of the ineffable, living God?"ᵃ

¹¹Peter said to him, "Go in and say to Simon in the midstᵃ of his followers, 'Peter says to you, "Come out in public, for because of you I came to Rome, perverse disturber of simple souls!" ' "

¹²Immediately, the dog ran in, rushed into the midstᵃ of the people around Simon, raised his front feet, and said in a very loud voice, ¹³"You, Simon! To you Peter, Christ's servant, who stands at the door, says, 'Come out in public! ¹⁴Because of you I have come to Rome, you most perverse deceiver of simple souls.' "

¹⁵When Simon heard this and saw the incredible sight, he forgot the words with which he had deceived those who surrounded him; everyone <else> was stunned, too.

10 When Marcellus saw this, he went out to the door. ²Casting himself at Peter's feet, he said, "Peter, I embrace your feet. Holy servant of the holy God, I have sinned greatly, but do not punish my sins! ³If that true faith in Christ whom you preach is in you, if you remember his commandments to hate no one,ᵃ to be harmful

---

9:15 • *everyone <else> was stunned:* Vouaux (1922: 291 n. 1) notes the similarity of this incident to Acts 8:13; see also AcPetVerc 12:8, 15; 22:17.

to no one, as I have learned from Paul, your fellow apostle, do not call to mind my faults. [4]But pray for me to the Lord, the Holy Son of God, whom I have provoked to wrath because I have persecuted his servants! [5]So please plead on my behalf, like a good steward of God. [6]Don't hand me over to eternal fire with the sins of Simon, who swayed me so far that I set up a statue of him with an inscription of this sort: 'To Simon, the young god.'

[7]"If I thought, Peter, that money would persuade <you>, I would give all my property—despising it, I would give it to you in order to profit my soul.[a] [8]If I had sons, I would consider them nothing,[a] if only I could have faith in the Lord. [9]I confess that he would not have seduced me if he had said that he is the Power of God. [10]For all that, I tell you, dearest Peter, I was not worthy to hear you, servant of God, nor was I established in faith in God, which is in Christ; this is why I was scandalized. [11]So I ask you not to be offended by what I am about to say: [12]Christ, our Lord, whom you preach in truth, said to your fellow apostles in your presence, 'If you have faith like a grain of mustard, if you say to this mountain, "Move," it will move immediately.'[a] [13]Peter, this Simon called you unfaithful because you doubted on the water.[a] [14]I also heard that <Jesus> said, 'Those who are with me do not understand me.'[a] [15]So if you, on whom he placed his hands, whom he also chose, and with whom he worked marvels, doubted— [16]<then> I repent, since I have this evidence; and I take refuge in your prayers. [17]Lift up my soul, for I have fallen from our Lord and from his promise. [18]But I believe that he will be merciful to me since I repent, because the omnipotent one is faithful to forgive me my sins."

[19]Peter said in a loud voice, "To you, our Lord, be glory and renown, omnipotent God, Father of our Lord Jesus Christ: to you be praise, glory and honor for ever and ever, Amen. [20]Since you have now fully strengthened and established us in yourself, in the sight of all these onlookers, holy Lord, confirm Marcellus and place your peace in him and in his house today! [21]Whatever is lost or

10:7 [a]Cf. Mk 8:36; Mt 16:26; Lk 9:25

10:8 [a]Cf. Mt 10:37; Lk 14:26

10:12 [a]Cf. Mk 11:23; Mt 17:20; 21:21; Lk 17:6; APa 10.3:5

10:13 [a]Cf. APeVer 7:9; Mt 14:28–33

10:14 [a]Cf. AJn 92:3

10:6 • *'To Simon, the young god' (Simoni juveni deo)*: Possibly "new god," if *iuvenis* translates νέος (cf. *Vit. Aberc.* 134). But neither phrase fits the recovered inscription as closely as Justin's Σίμωνι δεωσάγκτῳ (*1 Apol.* 26.2; Goodspeed, 1914: 43) as reported in Eusebius *Hist eccl.* 2.13: Σίμωνι θεῷ ἁγίῳ (*Simoni deo sancto*).
10:10 • *in faith in God, which is in Christ (in fide Dei quae est in Christo)*: See note on AcPetVerc 7:26.
10:15 • *if you:* The "you" here is plural, i.e., Peter and the other apostles (see v. 12).
  • *on whom he placed his hands (quibus et manus imposuit)*: This statement suggests some sort of dominical "ordination" of the apostles, not attested in the NT gospels; but see Acts 6:6; 8:17–19; 13:3; 19:6; 1 Tim 4:14; 5:22; 2 Tim 1:6; Heb 6:2.

10:22 ªCf. Zc 13:7;
Mk 14:27; Mt 26:31

11:3 ª» APeVer 6:13

11:8 ªCf. Lk 4:35

wandering, you alone are able to restore it all. ²²We pray to you, Lord, shepherd of sheep that once were scattered³ but now are brought together by you, accept Marcellus thus also as one of your lambs, and no longer allow him to revel in error or ignorance, but receive him into the number of your sheep. ²³Now, Lord, accept the one who entreats you with anguish and tears.

11 After Peter had said these things and embraced Marcellus, he turned to the crowd that stood near him. ²He noticed someone in the crowd smiling—someone in whom there was the most wicked demon. ³So Peter said to him, "Whoever you are who smiled,³ show yourself publicly to everyone standing here!"

⁴Hearing this, the youth rushed into the atrium of the house. ⁵Crying out with a loud voice, and throwing himself against the wall, he said, "Peter, a great confrontation is taking place between Simon and the dog you sent. ⁶Simon is telling the dog, 'Deny that I am here!' and the dog says <even> more to him than you commanded. ⁷Yet <I know that> after he completes the mystery that you assigned him, he will die at your feet."

⁸Peter said, "You too, whatever demon you are—in the name of our Lord Jesus Christ, leave the youth without hurting him!³ Show yourself to everyone standing here!" ⁹When it heard this, it left the youth, and, taking hold of a statue set up in the atrium, it kicked it to pieces.

¹⁰Now, this was a statue of Caesar. Marcellus struck his brow at the sight <of this>, and said to Peter, "A great offense has been committed. ¹¹If Caesar gets to know of this through any of his spies, he will inflict a great punishment on us."

¹²Peter said to him, "I see that you are not the same as you were a moment ago! ¹³For <then> you said you were ready to choose to

11:2 • *smiling* (*subridentem*): See note on AcPetVerc 6:13.
• *someone in whom … wicked demon:* Cf. Philostratus *Vit. Apoll.* 4.20. On the demon's "smiling" (*subridentem*) see note on AcPetVerc 6:13: the demons, too, have special knowledge (cf. Mark 1:24; 3:11; Luke 4:34, 41).
11:3 • *Show yourself publicly:* The repetition of this command in v. 8 suggests that the intervening material has been inserted to connect this incident to the larger narrative.
11:11 • *spies:* Bremmer (1998b: 19) notes that the word used here (*curiosi*) was applied to imperial agents only after 359 c.e., which might help to date the Latin translation.

11:9 *When it heard this, it left the youth:* This is Turner's reconstruction; the ms has "When the   youth heard this, he left."

spend all of your property in order to gain the salvation of your soul. [14]Still, if you are truly repentant, trusting in Christ with all your heart,[a] take up running water in your hands and pray to the Lord, and in his name sprinkle it over the fragments of the statue—and it shall be made whole, as before."

[15]Marcellus did not hesitate, but trusted with all his heart. [16]And before he took up the water in his hands, he looked up and said, "I have faith in you, Lord Jesus Christ. [17]Indeed, I am being shown by your apostle Peter whether I have proper faith in your holy name. [18]Therefore, I am taking up water in my hands, and in your name I am sprinkling these stones, so that the statue may be made whole as before. [19]So Lord, if it is your will that I remain in my body[a] and not suffer anything from Caesar, let this stone be whole as before." [20]Then he sprinkled water over the stone, and the statue was made whole.

[21]Peter gloried in the fact that he had not hesitated in petitioning the Lord. [22]Marcellus also was exalted in spirit, because such a remarkable first sign had been done through his hands. [23]So he had faith with all his heart[a] in the name of Jesus Christ, the Son of God, through whom all things impossible are possible.[b]

12 Inside, Simon said to the dog, "Tell Peter that I'm not here."

[2]The dog responded, in Marcellus's presence, "Most wicked and shameless man, most hostile to all who live and trust in Christ Jesus, a mute animal was sent to you and took on a human voice, so as to expose you and prove you a charlatan and a deceiver. [3]Have you thought all this time only to say, 'Say that I am not here?' [4]Were you not ashamed to utter your weak and useless cry against Peter, servant and apostle of Christ, as though you could hide from him who ordered me to speak to you face to face? [5]All this is taking place, not for your sake, but for those you were seducing and sending to perdition.[a] [6]So, then, you are accursed, as the enemy and corrupter of Christ's way of truth. [7]He will judge with undying fire the iniquities you have committed, and you shall be in the outer darkness."[a]

11:14 [a]Cf. APeVer 11:15, 23; 17:18; 22:1

11:15[a]» APeVer 11:14

11:19 [a]» APeVer 1:6

11:23[a]» APeVer 11:14

[b]Cf. Mk 10:27; Mt 19:26; Lk 1:27; 18:27

12:5 [a]Cf. APeVer 7:21

12:7 [a]Cf. Mt 8:12; 22:13; 25:30

11:14 • *take up running water (excipe desalientem aquam):* Cf. *Did.* 7:1 "in living water" (ἐν ὕδατι ζῶντι); AcThom 52:4.
12:2 • *took on a human voice (vocem humanem accipiens):* Cf. 2 Pet 2:16 Vulg. *hominis vocens loquens* (ἐν ἀνθρώπου φωνῇ φθεγξάμενον, of Balaam's ass; Num 22:21, 23, 28, 30–31).

11:16 *in his hands, he . . .,* following Turner's punctuation.

12:12 ª» APeVer 2:20
12:16 ª» APeVer 2:5
13:10 ª» APeBG 2:7

⁸When the dog had spoken these words, he left. ⁹The crowd followed him, so that Simon was bereft of a following—alone.

¹⁰<So now> the dog came to Peter, who was sitting with a crowd <who had come> to see Peter in person, and the dog reported what he had done with Simon. ¹¹The dog spoke these things to the angel and apostle of the true God: ¹²"Peter, you will have a great contest against Simon, the enemy of Christª and his servants. ¹³You will restore many to faith who were seduced by him. Because of this you will receive from God the <just> reward for your work."

¹⁴And when the dog had spoken these things to him, he fell at Peter's feet and gave up his spirit.

¹⁵As the large crowd watched the speaking dog with astonishment, some of them began to prostrate themselves at Peter's feet. ¹⁶But others said, "Show us another sign that we may trust in you as a servant of the living God.ª ¹⁷<After all,> Simon also produced many signs in our presence, and that's why we followed him."

13 Peter turned around and saw a herring hanging in the window. ²Taking it, he said to the people, "If you now see this swimming in water like a fish, will you be able to trust in him whom I preach?"

³They said unanimously, "We will certainly trust in you!"

⁴Now, nearby there was a tank where fish were swimming <around>; so he said, "In your name, Jesus Christ, which they still do not trust—before all of these: live and swim like a fish!" ⁵<So> he put the herring in the tank, and it came to life and began to swim.

⁶When the crowd saw the fish, <now> swimming.... ⁷But he made it do so not for that hour only, in case someone call it <merely> an illusion. Rather, he made it go on swimming. ⁸As a result, <the sight of it> drew crowds from all over—he showed that the herring had become a <living> fish; ⁹so that some of the people gave it bread, and <continued to> watch it <swimming around>. ¹⁰Because

---

12:10 • *to see Peter in person (ut viderunt faciem Petri)*, that is, "to see Peter's face."
12:14 • *and gave up his spirit (et deposuit spiritum)*: Cf. AcThom 41:2.
13:1 • *a herring (sardam)*: *sarda* can refer to several types of food fish preserved by drying or salting (LS, s.v. [p. 1631a]). Turner (126) suggests that the fish was a sign or ornament on a shop. Vouaux (1922: 309 n. 5) imagines a smoked herring. There is a similar story of the young Jesus in the Latin *Infancy Gospel of Thomas* 1.

12:11 *to the angel ... Peter*: Turner takes the dog's address to begin, "Angel and apostle of the true God, Peter...."

of this sight, many followed and had faith in the Lord, and they gathered day and night[a] at the house of Narcissus, the presbyter. [11]Peter explained the writings of the prophets and the things which our Lord Jesus Christ had done, both in word and in deed.

14 Marcellus was strengthened daily by the signs that he saw being brought about through Peter by the grace of Jesus Christ, which he had granted him. [2]Marcellus attacked Simon in his own house as he sat in the dining room. [3]Marcellus cursed him: "Most hostile and pestilential of men, corrupter of my soul and my household, who wishes to have me flee from Christ, the Lord, my savior!" [4]Laying hands on him, he ordered him thrown from his house.

[5]When the servants got an opportunity in this way, they flung insults at him; some struck him on the face, some even used a stick, and some a stone. [6]Others, who had offended their master because of him and had been chained for a long time, dumped out pots full of excrement over his head. [7]Yet others of their fellow servants, whom he had maligned to their master, abused him and said to him, [8]"Now we are giving you proper recompense by the will of God, who had pity on us and on our master."

[9]So when Simon had been soundly beaten and thrown out of the house, he ran to the house where Peter was staying. [10]At the house of the presbyter Narcissus, he stood at the door and called out, "Look! I am Simon. [11]So come down, Peter, and I will prove that you trust in a human being—a Jew and a carpenter's son."[a]

15 It was reported to Peter that Simon said these things, so Peter sent to him a woman who had a nursing infant, saying to her, [2]"Go down quickly, and you will see someone asking for me. [3]You are not to answer him at all; rather keep silent and listen to what the infant you are carrying will say to him." [4]So the woman went down.

14:11 [a]Cf. APeVer 7:19; 23:20; Mk 6:3; Mt 13:55; ATh 2:7

13:11 • *both in word and in deed (et verbo et factis):* Vouaux (1922: 311 n. 7), referring to Acts 1:1 (*facere et docere*, "to do and teach"), points to Eusebius *Hist. eccl.* 3.39.15, where the phrase τὰ ὑπὸ τοῦ Χριστοῦ ἢ λεχθέντα ἢ πραχθέντα ("things spoken and done by Christ") seems to refer to gospel literature. See also AcPetVerc 7:26; 17:38.

14:6 *chained for a long time:* So Turner; Lipsius "those who had fled their master."

15:12 ªCf. APeVer
8:22

16:1 ª» APeVer 6:13

16:5 ªCf. Jn 8:44

⁵The child, which she had nursed for seven months, could not yet talk, but it took on a manly voice and said to Simon, ⁶"O you who are dreadful before God and humans! O destruction of truth and most evil seed of corruption! O most unfruitful fruit of nature! ⁷Yet you appear only briefly and for a moment; afterward, eternal punishment waits for you. ⁸Born of a shameless father, you never send roots into the good, but rather into poison. ⁹You are an incredible offspring, forsaking every hope! <Even> when a dog exposed you, you were not disturbed! ¹⁰I, a <mere> 'infant,' am compelled by God to speak, and <still> you do not blush. ¹¹Yet even if you are unwilling, on the coming Sabbath day someone else will bring you to the Julian forum, so that the sort of person you are will be demonstrated in your own self. ¹²Now get away from the door through which the footsteps of the saints pass: you shall no longer corrupt the innocent soulsª you had overthrown and made sorrowful in their relations with Christ! ¹³Your most depraved nature will be revealed, and your machinations destroyed. ¹⁴<But> now I am speaking the last word to you: Jesus Christ says to you, 'Become speechless, compelled by my name, and leave Rome until the coming Sabbath.' "

¹⁵Immediately, having become speechless, he left Rome under compulsion and stayed in a stable.

¹⁶The woman returned with her infant to Peter, and reported to him and to the other brothers and sisters what the infant had said to Simon. ¹⁷So they magnified the Lord, who had revealed these things to human beings.

16 As night came on, while he remained awake Peter saw Jesus, clothed in splendor, smiling,ª and saying to him, ²"Already a great crowd of brothers and sisters has returned through me and through you who have done signs in my name. ³On the coming Sabbath you will have a contest of faith, and many more among the gentiles and the Jews shall be converted, in my name, to me—who was abused, mocked, and spat upon. ⁴For I, myself, will be with you when you ask for signs and prodigies, and you will convert many. ⁵You will have Simon opposing you through the works of his father,ª but all of his works will be proven to be spells and magical illusions. ⁶So do not let up now, and you will establish in my name whomever I send to you."

15:10 • *a <mere> "infant":* The "infant"—literally, one who cannot speak—is "compelled to speak."

15:12 *with Christ:* Turner "apart from Christ."
16:2 *through you who have done signs in my name:* Turner "through the signs you have done in my name."

[7]When it became light, he told the brothers and sisters that the Lord had appeared to him, and what he had instructed.

17 "Believe me, brothers and sisters, I put this Simon to flight from Judea, who was causing many evils with his magic spells[a]— [2]he was staying then in Judea with a woman of great worldly reputation, named Eubula. [3]She had in her possession a lot of gold, not to mention pearls of no small value. [4]Simon made his entrance secretly, with two <others just> like himself; none of the household saw those two, only Simon. [5]By making a spell, they carried off all of the woman's gold—but no one saw them <do it>. [6]When Eubula discovered what had happened, she began to torture <the various members of> her household, saying, [7]'You took advantage of this godly man's presence to despoil me, since you saw him whose name is the name of the Lord coming to me and honoring a simple woman.'

[8]"After fasting for three days and praying that this deed would be exposed, I saw in a vision Italicus and Antulus, whom I had instructed in the name of the Lord; [9]but also a boy, naked and in chains,[a] who gave me wheat bread and said to me, 'Peter, hold on for two more days, and you will see the mighty works of God. [10]As for the things lost from Eubula's house—Simon and two others carried them off, by using magic arts and creating an illusion. [11]You'll see them on the third day, at the ninth hour,[a] at the gate which leads to Neapolis— [12]<they'll be there,>selling to a goldsmith named Agrippinus a young satyr made of gold and weighing two pounds, which has a valuable stone in it. [13]You, of course, mustn't touch it, or you'll be polluted; but take some of the matron's servants with you. [14]Show them the goldsmith's shop, and then leave them <to do the rest>; because of this deed, many will believe in the name of the Lord. [15]The things they so often stole by their craft and malice shall be made clear <for all to see>.'

[16]"Well, when I heard this, I came to Eubula—and I found her sitting and weeping with torn clothes and disheveled hair. [17]I said to

---

17:6 • *what had happened*, literally, "this deed" (*hoc factum*).
17:9 • *the mighty works of God* (*magnalia dei*): See note on AcPetVerc 5:19.
17:11 • *Neapolis:* Vouaux (1922: 323 n. 6) points to the importance of this city after 70 c.e.

17:7 *the name of the Lord:* Lipsius and Gunderman suggest that some words have dropped out at the end of a page; Turner emends *nomen* ("name")

to *numen:* "whose name is the *Power* of God" (but note that in Acts 8:10 for ἡ δύναμις τοῦ θεοῦ Vulg. has not *numen Dei* but *virtus Dei*).

17:18 ª» APeVer 2:11

ᵇ» APeVer 11:14

17:25 ª» APeVer 2:5

17:31 ªCf. APeVer 28:12; Ac 10:42; Rom 14:9; 2Tm 4:1; 1Pt 4:5; AAnMt 14:5; ATh 28:8; 30:4

her, 'Eubula, get up from your mourning and make up your face! Arrange your hair, and put on clothes that are suitable to you! ¹⁸Pray to the Lord Jesus Christ, who judges every soul—for he is the Son of the invisible God, by whom you must be saved, if indeed you repent of your previous sinsª with your whole heart!ᵇ ¹⁹Receive power from him also! ²⁰Look, now the Lord says to you through me: 'Everything that you have lost you shall find.' ²¹After you have received these things, let him find you, so that you will be able to renounce this present world and seek eternal refreshment. ²²So listen to this: Let some of your household keep watch at the gate which leads to Neapolis. ²³On the day after tomorrow, at about the ninth hour <of the day> they will see two youths with a young satyr made of gold, weighing two pounds, and encased in gemstones—this is what a vision has shown me. ²⁴They will offer it for sale to a certain Agrippinus: he is familiar with <true> piety and with the faith which is in the Lord Jesus Christ. ²⁵Through Christ you will be shown that you must have faith in the living Godª and not in the magician Simon, who is an unstable demon. ²⁶He was willing to have you remain in mourning and to have your innocent household tortured; <but> he misled you with flattering talk alone. ²⁷He spoke of piety toward God with his mouth only, while he <himself> is filled with nothing but impiety. ²⁸When you intended to celebrate the festival—when you set out your idol and veiled it, and displayed all your precious things on a table—he brought in two youths, who were invisible. ²⁹None of your household could see them, because he worked magic spells: but they <are the ones> who stole your precious things. ³⁰But his machinations had no foundation, because my God disclosed it to me, so that you should not be deceived nor perish in Gehenna, no matter what impious and contrary things you have done against God— ³¹who is full of all truth and the just judge of the living and the dead.ª ³²There is no other hope of life for human beings except through him, through whom the things you lost are saved for you. ³³But now you must gain your <own> soul, also.'

17:18 • *by whom you must be saved* (*in quem te necesse est salvari*): Cf. Acts 4:12 "for there is no other name ... *by which we must be saved*" (ἐν ᾧ δεῖ σωθῆναι ἡμᾶς [v.l. ὑμᾶς B 1704 *pc*], Vulg. *in quo oporteat nos salvos fieri*); AcPaulThec 4:8 "the sonship granted through him, by which [one must] be saved."

17:23 • *the ninth hour <of the day>*, that is, at about 3 p.m.; see note on AcPetVerc 2:10.

17:24 • *and the faith which is in the Lord Jesus Christ* (*et fidei quae est in dominum Jesum Christum*): See note on AcPetVerc 7:26.

17:25 • *an unstable demon* (*instabili daemonio*): This phrase may be a deliberate rejection of Simon's claim (in AcPetMar 2[31]:13, 15) to be "the Standing One" (see Vouaux, 1922: 327 n. 7).

[34]"At that, she prostrated herself at my feet, saying, 'O man, who you are I do not know. [35]I received him [Simon] as a servant of God: whatever he asked of me for the care of the poor, I gave. [36]<I gave> a great deal through his hands, and I gave him many other things besides. [37]How has he been harmed by me, that he should strive against my house so?' "[a]

[38]"Peter said to her, 'Faith must be placed not in words but in actions and deeds![a] So, as it is begun, it must be continued.'

[39]"Then, leaving her, I went with two of Eubula's attendants and came to Agrippinus. [40]I said to him, 'Take a look, so that you will recognize these men. [41]Tomorrow, two young men will come to you wanting to sell a young satyr made of gold and set with stones—it belongs to their mistress. [42]You, then, take it as if to inspect it, and praise the craftsman's work. [43]<But be assured that> when these men arrive, God will guide the rest to its conclusion.'

[44]"On the next day, the matron's attendants and the youths who wished to sell to Agrippinus the young satyr made of gold came <as Peter had said> at about the ninth hour.[a] [45]They were <of course> apprehended at once, and it was reported to the matron. [46]Because she was upset, she went to the governor; in a loud voice she reported what had happened to her. [47]When Pompey, the governor, saw that this woman—who never went out in public—was so upset, he immediately rose from the tribunal, entered the praetorium, and commanded that they be brought and questioned. [48]Under torture they confessed that they followed in Simon's service: 'He enticed us with money,' they said. [49]When questioned further, they revealed that everything Eubula had lost was hidden underground in a cave beyond the gate, along with many other things.

[50]"When Pompey heard about this, he arose to go to the gate, and those two were shackled with double chains. [51]And <right then and there> Simon was coming in at the gate, looking for them— they were late <for their appointment with him>. [52]What he saw was a large crowd coming <towards him>, and those two bound in chains. [53]Immediately he understood <what must have happened>, and made off in flight; he has not been seen in Judea from then until now.

17:37 [a]Cf. ATh 128:2

17:38 [a]Cf. APeVer 7:26

17:44 [a]» APeVer 2:10

17:38 • *Peter said to her:* Vouaux (1922: 329 n. 11) suggests that the shift to third-person narrative may be a remnant of an earlier form; but such slips appear elsewhere in V, esp. in speeches (see 8:1–5; 21:8).

17:47 • *Pompey:* Pompeius Longinus was legate in Jerusalem until 83 c.e.; but the author may have had the more famous general in mind (Vouaux, 1922: 331 n. 3).

18:5 ^a» APeVer 2:24

⁵⁴"As for Eubula, after she recovered all her goods, she gave them for the service of the poor: she <now> had faith in the Lord Jesus Christ, and she was strengthened <by it>. ⁵⁵Despising and renouncing this world, she gave to widows and orphans, and after clothing the poor for a long time, she received her rest.

⁵⁶"These things, dearest brothers and sisters, are <what was done> done in Judea; and so it was that was the one who is called 'the angel of Satan' was expelled from there.

18 "Dearest and best-loved brothers and sisters, let us fast and pray by turns to the Lord. ²The one who drove him from there is able to remove him from this place as well. ³He gives us power to resist him and his magic spells, and to prove that he is the angel of Satan. ⁴On the Sabbath, our Lord shall bring him, even against his will, into the Julian forum. ⁵So let us bend our knees^a to Christ, who hears us, even if we have not called out—he is the one who sees us, even if he is not seen by these eyes, yet he is with us. ⁶If we wish, he does not withdraw from us. ⁷So let us purify our souls of every evil temptation, and God will not depart from us: if we merely beckon with our eyes, he is with us."

19 After these things were spoken by Peter, Marcellus came in also. ²He said, "Peter, I have cleansed my whole house of the traces of Simon for you, and I have rooted out his wicked dust. ³I took up water, and, invoking the holy name of Jesus Christ, together with the rest of my servants who belong to him, I sprinkled my whole house along with every dining room—all the colonnades and even the exterior around the doorway. ⁴I said, 'I know that you, Lord Jesus Christ, are pure and untouched by every impurity, so that my enemy and foe is expelled from your sight.' ⁵Now, most blessed one, I have ordered the widows and the elderly to assemble with you in the communal house so they can pray with us. ⁶They shall receive,

---

17:55 • *she received her rest:* Vouaux (1922: 333 n. 7) rightly notes that the temporal perspective is incongruous in the present context, and conjectures therefore that Peter's speech has been transposed from direct narrative.

17:56 • *'the angel of Satan':* This title, of course, establishes a contrast with Peter, who is "the angel of God" (cf. 2 Cor 12:7).

19:6 • *a single gold piece:* This specific gift, perhaps inspired by Job 42:11 (see LXX and Vulg.), is a concrete demonstration of the patron-client relationship between Christ and the faithful; see also AcPetVerc 23:1.

19:5 *in the communal house:* Turner "in the house which has been cleansed."

in the name of their service, a single gold piece, so that they may truly be called servants of Christ. Everything else is prepared for the service. [7]I ask you therefore, most blessed Peter: put your seal on their entreaties, so that you also might adorn their prayers on my behalf. [8]Let's go, then, taking with us both Narcissus and any of the brothers and sisters who are here."

[9]Peter acquiesced to his simplicity and went forth with him and the rest of the brothers and sisters to fulfill his desire.

20 Peter entered and saw one of the elderly women, a blind widow, along with her daughter, who was giving her a hand and leading her into Marcellus's house. [2]Peter said to her, "Come near, mother! From this day on, Jesus, through whom we have unapproachable light,[a] whom the darkness cannot conceal, gives you his right hand.[b] [3]He says to you through me, 'Open your eyes, see, and walk on your own!'" [4]Immediately, the widow saw Peter placing his hand on her.

[5]Then Peter entered the dining room and saw the gospel being read. [6]Rolling it up,[a] he said to them, "You who trust and hope in Christ, know how the holy scriptures of our Lord must be proclaimed. [7]We wrote these things, as far as we have understood them, by his grace. [8]Although they may still seem feeble to you, they are nevertheless conveyed as fittingly as it is possible to bring them to human flesh. [9]We ought, therefore, to know first God's will or goodness. [10]Since at that time error was pervasive, and many thousands were sinking to destruction, the Lord in his mercy was moved to show himself in another form and to be seen in the image of a man. [11]Concerning him neither the Jews nor we were able to be enlightened adequately, for each of us saw just what he could, according to his ability to see.

[12]"Now, I will explain to you what was just read to you. [13]When our Lord Jesus Christ wished me to see his majesty on the holy mountain and I and the sons of Zebedee saw the splendor of his glory, I fell down as though dead. [14]I closed my eyes, and I heard his voice such as I cannot describe, so that I thought I would be deprived of sight by his splendor.[a] [15]Scarcely breathing, I said to

20:2 [a]Cf. 1Tm 6:16
[b]» APeBG 1:11
20:6 [a]Cf. Lk 4:20
20:14 [a]Cf. Mt 17:6

20:7–8 • *We wrote these things . . . :* The precise translation of these lines remains uncertain. See Hilhorst, 1998: 158.

20:12 • *what was just read:* What follows is loosely based on the NT gospel accounts of the transfiguration (Matt 17:1–8; Mark 9:2–8; Luke 9:28–36); Matthew's version has contributed some distinctive details. See also 2 Pet 1:16–18; AcJohn 90:1–12.

20:16 ªCf. Mt 17:7
20:19 ªCf. Is 53:4
ᵇCf. Jn 10:38; 17:21;
AJn 100:6
20:20 ªCf. Col 2:9
20:26 ªCf. IPol 3:2
21:1 ª» APeVer 2:10

myself, 'Perhaps my Lord wanted to bring me here in order to deprive me of sight.' [16]I said, 'This too is your will. I will not object, Lord.' He gave me his hand and lifted me up.[a] [17]When I stood, I saw him again in a way that I was able to apprehend.

[18]"So then, dearest brothers and sisters, just as God, who is merciful, has borne our weaknesses and carried our offenses, [19]as the prophet said, 'He bears our sins and suffers for us, but we thought him to be in anguish and enduring blows,'[a] for he is in the Father and the Father is in him.[b] [20]He is himself also the fullness of all majesty,[a] who has shown us all his goodness. [21]He ate and drank for our sake, although he was neither hungry nor thirsty. [22]He also bore and suffered shameful things for our sakes. He died and rose again because of us. [23]He who both defended me when I sinned and strengthened me by his greatness will console you so that you will love him. [24]He is both great and very small, beautiful and ugly, young and old, appearing in time and wholly invisible in eternity. [25]He is the one whom human hand has not held and the one who will be touched by his servants, whom flesh has not seen and now <is seen>, who is not heard but now is understood. [26]The word heard is now also like us, yet a stranger to suffering:[a] never before chastened but now chastened, the one who is before the world and is comprehended within time, [27]the great beginning of all rule and handed over to rulers, beautiful but humble among us, ugly to see but foreseeing. [28]This Jesus you cling to, brothers and sisters, as the Door, Light, Way, Bread, Water, Life, Resurrection, Refreshment, Pearl, Treasure, Seed, Abundance, Mustard Seed, Vine, Plough, Grace, Faith, Word. [29]This one is all things, and there is no other greater than he. To him be praise, world without end."

21 When the ninth hour[a] was completed, they stood up to offer a prayer. [2]It happened that some of the old widows who, unknown to Peter, were sitting there blind and not believing suddenly called out to Peter, "We sit here together, Peter, hoping and believing in Christ. [3]We ask you therefore, lord Peter, just as you have made one of us see, grant us also his mercy and kindness."

[4]Peter responded, "If there is in you the faith which is in Christ,

20:28 • *Door, Light,…*: This list of titles draws on the parable tradition.
21:4 • *the faith which is in Christ (fides qaue est in Christo)*: See note on AcPetVerc 17:24.

20:18 *So then,…*: The final paragraph of this speech appears in a slightly expanded form in *Vit.*
Aberc. ff. 133–34.
21:2 *not believing*: Turner "not having risen."

if it is confirmed in you, see with your understanding what you do not see with your eyes![a] [5]Although your ears are closed, let them be open within your mind, for these eyes will again be closed, which see nothing other than men, cattle, mute animals, stones, and pieces of wood, but not all eyes see Jesus Christ. [6]Now, Lord let your sweet and holy name come to the aid of these women! Touch their eyes—for you are able—that they may see by their own light!"

[7]When everyone had prayed, the dining room where they were shone with bright light as when the dawn comes, and with such a light as is usually seen <only> in the clouds. [8]Yet it was not like the light of the day, but an ineffable, invisible light which no one can describe,[a] a light which illuminated us so that we were beside ourselves[b] with bewilderment and called out to the Lord, [9]"Lord, have mercy on us, your servants. Give us, Lord, what we are able to bear, for this we can neither see nor bear."

[10]As we lay there, only those widows who were blind stood up. The bright light which appeared to us entered into their eyes and made them see. [11]Peter said to them, "Tell what you saw!"

[12]They said, "We saw an old man whose beauty we cannot describe to you." [13]Others said, "A young man in adolescence." Others said, "We saw a boy gently touching our eyes.[a] That's how our eyes were opened."

[14]Peter magnified the Lord, saying, "You only are Lord, God! What great lips we would need to offer you praise, if we were to give you thanks according to your mercy! [15]Therefore, brothers and sisters, just as I told you a little while ago, 'God remains greater than our understanding,' so we have learned from these elderly widows how they have each seen the Lord in a different way.

22 After he had exhorted them all to understand the Lord with their whole hearts,[a] he began to serve the Lord's virgins, along with Marcellus and the other brothers and sisters, and he rested until morning. [2]Marcellus said to them, "Holy, inviolate virgins of the

21:4 [a]» APeBG 2:17

21:8 [a]Cf. ATh 27:13

[b]Cf. ATh 1:2

21:13 [a]Cf. AJn 88:6; 89:1

22:1 [a]» APeVer 11:14

21:8–10 • *illuminated us:* It is unclear whether the shift to first-person narration should be seen as evidence of a separate source or is the result of carelessness on the part of the author or translator (Vouaux, 1922: 352 n. 2).
22:1 • *he rested until morning:* Cf. PsClemRec 1.74.

21:7 *… in the clouds:* Lipsius adds a reference to lightning from *Vit. Aberc.* ff. 136–37.

21:15 *we have learned (didicimus)* is corrected from *tredecim* ("thirteen") (so Lipsius).

22:16 ᵃCf. 2Tm 2:13;
APaMar 2:12–13

22:17 ᵃCf. Mt 26:51;
Mk 14:47; Lk 22:49–
50; Jn 18:10–11

ᵇCf. ATh 11:3–5

Lord, listen! ³You have a place to stay, for to whom do these things called 'mine' belong, if not to you? ⁴Don't leave here, but take refreshment, for on tomorrow's Sabbath Simon will have a contest with Peter, the holy one of God. ⁵Just as the Lord has always been with him, so also now may Christ the Lord stand by him, because he is his apostle. ⁶Peter, moreover, has continued to taste nothing; he extends his fast so that he may overcome the evil enemy and persecutor of the Lord's truth. ⁷Look, my servants have come, and they are announcing that they have seen bleachers constructed in the forum and a crowd saying, 'Tomorrow, at first light, two Jews will dispute about how God should be addressed.' ⁸Now, let's keep vigil until morning, entreating and pleading with our Lord, Jesus Christ, that he might listen to our prayers for Peter."

⁹After Marcellus had fallen asleep for a moment and awakened <again>, he said to Peter, "Peter, apostle of Christ, let's go on to our objective boldly! ¹⁰Just now, when I fell asleep for a moment, I saw <you> sitting in a high place with a large crowd in front of you. ¹¹There was a most hideous woman dancing, who looked like an Ethiopian, not like an Egyptian, but totally black. ¹²She was wrapped in filthy rags, and had an iron collar on her neck and chains on her hands and feet. ¹³As you watched, you said to me in a loud voice, 'Marcellus, this dancer is the whole power of Simon and his god. Cut off her head!' ¹⁴But I said to you, 'Brother Peter, I am a senator from a great family, and I have never stained my hands. I have never killed even a sparrow.' ¹⁵When you heard this, you began to cry out further, 'Come, our true sword, Jesus Christ! ¹⁶Not only cut off this demon's head, but also cut all of her members to pieces in the presence of all these whom I have approved for your service.'ᵃ ¹⁷Immediately someone who was like you, Peter, and held a sword,ᵃ cut her all to pieces, so that I stared with great amazement at the two of you—at you and at the one who cut up that demon—who were so similar.ᵇ ¹⁸Now that I have woken up, I have reported these signs from Christ to you."

¹⁹When Peter heard these things, he was again filled with courage because of what Marcellus had seen—for the Lord always provides for his own. ²⁰Thus cheered and refreshed by these words, he got up to go to the forum.

22:13 *the whole power (omnis virtus) is corrected
from omnes viri ("all the men") (so Lipsius).*

23:1 ªCf. APeVer 19:6
23:3 ª» APeVer 4:10
23:15 ªCf. Ac 8:18–19
23:17 ª» APeVer 2:5
23:20 ª» APeVer 14:11

23 The brothers and sisters together with all who were in Rome assembled, each paying a single gold piece[a] to take a seat. [2]Senators, prefects, and officials flocked in as well. [3]When Peter arrived and stood in their midst,[a] they all exclaimed, "Show us, Peter, who your God is, or what his greatness is, that has given you such faith! [4]Don't be grudging toward the Romans; they are lovers of the gods. [5]We have evidence from Simon. Let us have yours also! You two show us whom we really ought to trust." [6]While they said these things, Simon also arrived. [7] He stood confused at Peter's side and gazed at him in particular.

[8]After a long silence, Peter said, "Romans, you be our true judges! [9]I say that I have trusted in the living and true God; I offer to give you evidences of him. [10]These proofs are already known to me, as many among you can also testify. [11]You see that this fellow is constrained in this manner—he is silent about the fact that I drove him out of Judea because of the deceptions he practiced through his magic arts on Eubula, an honorable and very simple woman. [12]Since he was driven from there by me, he has come here thinking that he could hide among you. [13]But look! Now he stands face to face with me. Speak, Simon! [14]Didn't you throw yourself down at my feet and at Paul's in Jerusalem when you saw the healings which were done by our hands? [15]Didn't you say, 'I beg you, take as much payment as you want from me, if I too can lay on hands and perform such wonders'?[a] [16]And when we heard this from you, we cursed you, <saying,> 'Do you expect to tempt us with the desire for money?' Do you now fear nothing? [17]My name is Peter, because the Lord Christ deigned to call me 'prepared for everything,' for I have faith in the living God,[a] through whom I will put down your magic. [18]Now, let him do in your presence one of the marvels which he used to do. [19]Then won't you believe me and what I have just said about him?"

[20]Simon, however, said this: "Do you dare to speak of Jesus of Nazareth, the son of a carpenter and a carpenter himself,[a] whose birth is placed in Judea? [21]Listen out, Peter! These Romans are

23:8 • *Romans (Viri Romani):* See also AcPetVerc 23:22; 28:10, 22, 31, 38, 70; 31:11 (A Ἄνδρες Ῥωμαῖοι); and, with the vocative "O," in 24:13; 28:47.
23:14 • *and at Paul's:* Many interpreters see the presence of Paul in this encounter as a secondary insertion. In the Syriac *Preaching of Simon Cephas,* Peter says, "Simon, you threw yourself at my feet and at those of the other apostles" (Bedjan, 1890: 20); see Poupon, 1988: 4372.
23:17 • *"prepared for everything":* The Latin pun (*Petrus-paratus*) may replace a derivation of the name based on the Greek; cf. Matt 16:17–19.

23:22 ᵃ» APeVer 23:8

24:3 ᵃCf. Is 53:2

24:4 ᵃCf. Hb 1:1–2

ᵇCf. Is 9:6

ᶜCf. Mt 1:18–19; Lk
1:34–35

24:6 ᵃCf. Is 7:14

24:7 ᵃCf. Asc.Isa.
11.14

24:9 ᵃCf. Dan 2:34

24:10 ᵃCf. Ps 118:22;
Mk 12:10; Mt 21:42;
Lk 20:17; Ac 4:11;
1Pt 2:7

24:11 ᵃCf. Is 28:16

24:12 ᵃCf. Dan 7:13;
Mk 13:26; Mt 24:30;
Lk 21:27

24:13 ᵃCf. APeMar
2(31):7

ᵇ» APeVer 23:8

24:14 ᵃCf. APeVer
7:21

ᵇCf. Rm 16:25

ᶜCf. APeMar
8(37):2–5

intelligent people; they're no fools." ²²And turning to the crowd he said, "Romans,ᵃ can God be born? crucified? ²³Whoever has a 'lord' cannot <himself> be God!" ²⁴When he had said this, many said <in reply>, "You have spoken well, Simon!"

24 But Peter came back at him: "A curse on your words against Christ! ²Are you so arrogant as to say this when the prophet says, 'Who could tell his kind?' ³or when another <time the> prophet says, 'We saw him, and he possessed neither beauty nor grace'?ᵃ ⁴and, 'In the last timesᵃ a boy will be bornᵇ from the Holy Spirit. His mother knows not a man,ᶜ nor does anyone say he is his father.' ⁵Again he says, 'She has given birth and not given birth.' ⁶And again, 'Is it a small thing for you to contend?' and, 'Behold! A virgin conceives in her womb.'ᵃ ⁷Another prophet, giving honor to the Father, says, 'We have neither heard her voice nor has a midwife entered.'ᵃ ⁸Yet another prophet says, 'He was not born from the womb of a woman, but he descended from a heavenly place,' ⁹and, 'A stone was cut without hands and has struck down all the kingdoms,'ᵃ ¹⁰and, 'A stone which the builders rejected, this was placed in the head of the corner.'ᵃ ¹¹He also calls him a stone 'chosen, and precious.'ᵃ ¹²Again the prophet says of him, 'Behold! I saw coming on a cloud one like a son of man.'ᵃ ¹³What more besides?ᵃ O Romans,ᵇ if you were acquainted with the prophetic scriptures, I would expound everything to you. ¹⁴Because of these <scriptures> it was necessary that the kingdom of Godᵃ also should come to completion through a mystery.ᵇ However, these things will be revealed to you later.ᶜ ¹⁵As for you, Simon, do any of those things by which you used to seduce them, and I will undo it by my Lord Jesus Christ."

¹⁶Simon grew bold. "If," he said, "the prefect permits!"

23:23 • *Whoever has a 'lord' (Qui dominum habet)…:* The argument is reminiscent of the dispute in Mark 12:35–37 (Matt 22:41–46; Luke 20:41–44) about "David's son" (cf. Ps 110:1).
24:1 • *A curse on* translates *anatema*.
24:2 • *his kind* translates *genus eius* (cf. Isa 53:8 Vulg. *generationem eius*).
24:5 • *"She has given birth and not given birth"*: This saying is attributed to Ezekiel by Tertullian (*De carn.* 22); but cf. Clement of Alexandria *Strom.* 7.16; Epiphanius *Pan.* 30.30; also *Thund.* (NHC VI,2) 13,19–20 "I am the wife and the virgin."
24:6 • *Is it a small thing…?* An abbreviated quotation of Isa 7:13, perhaps through a copyist's error; see Turner, 1931: 129.
24:13 • *I would expound everything:* It is likely that the author has made use of a testimony collection rather than quote directly from the OT. Hilhorst (1998: 159–60) suggests rendering this problematic sentence thus: "According to which (sc. prophetical writings), <which expressed themselves> in a symbolic way (*per mysterium*), it was also necessary that the kingdom of God should be completed."

25 The prefect wanted to show patience toward the two men, so that he would not seem to be acting impiously. ²Therefore he brought forward one of the boys from his own household and said this to Simon: "Take this one, and put him to death." ³To Peter he said, "You then revive him!" ⁴The prefect said to the people, "It is for you to judge which of them is acceptable to God: the one who brings death or the one who brings life."[a] ⁵Immediately, Simon spoke into the boy's ear; he made him silent, and caused him to die without <so much as> a cry.

⁶As the people began to murmur, one of the widows who was resting at Marcellus's house called out from behind the crowd, "Peter, servant of God, my son has died—the only one I had!"[a]

⁷The people made way for her[a] and led her up to Peter. ⁸She prostrated herself at his feet saying, "I had just the one son, who provided my livelihood with his shoulders. ⁹He lifted me up; he carried me about. And now that he's dead, who will offer me a hand?"

¹⁰Peter said to her, "Go with these witnesses and bring your son, so that when they see they will be able to believe that he is raised by the power of God." ¹¹And when she heard this, she collapsed.

¹²Then Peter said to the young men, "We need some youths, especially those who desire to have faith." ¹³At once thirty of them came forward, prepared either to carry her or to bring in her dead son.[a]

¹⁴Since the widow had only just recovered herself, the youths lifted her up. ¹⁵She tore her hair and her face as she cried out, "Look, my son, Christ's servant is sending for you!"

¹⁶The youths who came checked the boy's nostrils <to see> if he really had died. ¹⁷Seeing that he was truly dead, they consoled the old woman, saying, "If you wish, mother, and you trust in Peter's

25:4 ªCf. PsClemR 3.60; PsClemH 2.34

25:6 ªCf. Lk 7:12–15

25:7 ªCf. APeVer 27:2; 28:2

25:13 ªCf. APa 4.1:15 (PHeid 30)

25:2 • *one of the boys* (*alumni*): *alumnus* originally referred to a foster-child, but should probably be understood here as a slave born in the household (Vouaux, 1922: 372 n. 1).
25:8 • *my livelihood* (*alimentum*), literally, "nourishment, sustenance," but with extended meanings (in Vulg. only at 1 Tim 6:8, for διατροφή). Poupon (1997: 1094) suggests emending to *adiumentum* ("help, aid, assistance"), which would shift the imagery to physical support more consistently.

25:11 *When she heard this*, reading *illa* ("she") for *ille* ("he," i.e., Simon) (so Lipsius) and *audiens* ("hearing") for *videns* ("seeing") (so Turner).
25:16 *the boy's nostrils*: P.Oxy. 849 can be translated from this point.
25:17 *the old woman*: So P.Oxy. 849; V *matrem ipsius* ("his mother").
"*If you wish … to you*": P.Oxy. 849; V "If you truly have faith in Peter's God, we will carry him and take him to Peter, so that by reviving him he will return him to you."

26:9 ª» APaTh 9:2

27:2 ªCf. APeVer 25:7; 28:2

27:4 ªCf. Mt 7:7; Lk 11:9; Mk 11:24; Mt 21:22; Jn 14:13–14; 15:7; 16:23

God, we will carry him and go there, so that by raising him he will return him to you."

26 While they were saying these things, the prefect in the forum stared at Peter and said, "What do you say? ²Look, Peter, my servant lies dead, whom even the emperor holds dear. ³I did not spare him, even though I have other young men with me; but I was willing to have this boy die because I wished to test whether you and your god are true."

⁴Peter said, "God is not to be tested or examined, Agrippa, but when he is loved and entreated he listens to those who are worthy. ⁵Now, however, since my God and Lord, Jesus Christ, is being tested among you, he who has performed such great signs and prodigies through me for the conversion of his sinners— ⁶<I ask> now, in the sight of all: Lord, through my word, raise up by your power the one whom Simon killed by his touch."

⁷Then Peter said to the boy's master, "Go, take his right hand, and you shall have him alive and walking with you!"

⁸Agrippa, the prefect, ran up to the boy, and taking his hand he revived him. ⁹When the crowd saw it, they all called out, "God is one!ª The God of Peter is one!"

27 Meanwhile the widow's son was also brought in on a litter by the youths. ²The people made way for themª and guided them to Peter. ³Peter raised his eyes toward heaven, extended his hands, and spoke in this manner: ⁴"Holy Father of your Son Jesus Christ, who has granted us your power so that we ask through you and get <what we ask for>,ª ⁵we disdain all the things that are in the world, and we follow you alone, who are seen by few but wish to be known by many. ⁶Shine around us Lord! Illumine! Appear! Revive the son of the elderly widow, who is not able to support herself without her

---

26:9 • *God of Peter:* For "God of *an apostle's name*," see also 27:10.
27:3 • *raised his eyes toward heaven, extended his hands:* These are the usual gestures associated with prayer in contemporary Judaism and Christianity.

26:2 *because I wished to test … are true:* So P.Oxy. 849; V "but believing in you and the god you preach whether you are certain and true."

26:4 *Agrippa:* V omits the name.
    entreated: V adds "from the soul."
26:5 *Now, however:* P. Oxy. 849 breaks off here.

son! [7]Taking on the voice of Christ, my Lord, I say to you, 'Young man, arise and walk with your mother, for so long as you are useful to her! [8]Later you will be free for me, serving in another capacity—as deacon of the bishop.' "

[9]Immediately the dead man got up. [10]When the crowd saw it, they were astonished—the people called out, "You are God, the Savior! You, the God of Peter![a] The invisible God and Savior!" [11]They talked among themselves, truly astonished at the power of a man who called upon his Lord by his word, and they accepted it for their sanctification.

28 As the report flew throughout the whole city, a senator's mother arrived.[a] [2]She pressed through the middle[a] of the crowd and fell at Peter's feet, saying, [3]"I have been informed by my people that you are the servant of a merciful God, and that you share his grace with all who desire this light. [4]So now, share <this> light with my son as well, because I know that you are grudging toward no one. [5]When a matron entreats you, <surely> you will not turn away."

[6]Peter said to her, "Do you have faith in my God, through whom your son shall be resurrected?"

[7]The mother spoke with a loud voice and tears, "I have faith, Peter. I have faith."

[8]All the people exclaimed, "Give the mother her son!"

[9]But Peter said, "Let him be brought here before everyone present!" [10]Turning to the people, Peter said, "Romans,[a] I also am one of you — a flesh-bearing human being and a sinner.[b] [11]I, however, have obtained mercy. So do not stare at me, as though I were doing what

27:10 [a]» APeVer 26:8
28:1 [a]Cf. APh 28–29; 80–85
28:2 [a]» APeVer 4:10
28:10 [a]» APeVer 23:8
[b]Cf. Ac 14:15
28:11 [a]Cf. Ac 3:12; PsClemR 10.70

27:7 • *voice* (*vox*) may refer to a word or saying of Christ.
• *I say to you, "Young man, arise"* (*dico tibi: Iuvenis, surge*): Cf. Luke 7:14 Vulg. *Adolescens, tibi dico, surge.*
27:8 • *free for me*, that is, after the death of the young man's mother.
28:2 • *She pressed through the middle* (*misit se per mediam*): There may be a deliberate contrast between the humbler suppliants (the widow, in 25:7; the youths bearing the widow's son, in 27:2), for whom the crowd "makes way," and this senator's wife, pushing her way, it seems, through the crowd (see also *misit se per medium* in 28:15).

27:7 *deacon of the bishop:* So Flamion (1909: 275 n. 7) and Turner *diaconi episcopi sorte* ("as deacon of the bishop"); V has *diaconi ac episcopi te* ("deacon and bishop"). See Phil 1:1; and note the strong connection between deacon and bishop in Hippolytus *Apost. trad.* 9.2 "[the deacon] is not or-dained for a priesthood, but for the service of the bishop. . . ."
27:8 *serving in another capacity* (*altariis ministrans*): So Usener; Lipsius and Vouaux *altius ministrans* ("serving in a higher ministry"); Turner *ad latus* ("at my side").

28:12 [a]» APeVer 17:31
28:15 [a]» APeVer 4:10
[b]» APaTh 5:1
28:22 [a]» APeVer 23:8
28:23 [a]» APeVer 2:5
28:31 [a]» APeVer 23:8

I do by my own power.[a] [12]I do it, rather, by my Lord Jesus Christ, who is the judge of the living and the dead.[a] [13]Because I have faith in him and have been sent by him, I am confident to call upon him to raise the dead. [14]Therefore, woman, you go, too! Have your son brought here and raised!"

[15]The woman pressed through the middle[a] of the crowd and went out into the open street, running with great joy.[a] [16]With faith in her mind, she entered her house and had him carried to the forum by her servants. [17]She told her servants to put caps on their heads and to walk in front of the bier. [18]<In fact,> she had them carry all that was prepared for her son's body in front of his bier, so that when Peter saw it he would have pity on the body and on her.

[19]While they were all lamenting, she arrived back at the multitude. [20]A throng of senators and matrons followed in order to see the marvels of God, since Nicostratus, who had died, was very noble and greatly loved in the senate. [21]When they brought him in, they placed him in front of Peter.

[22]Peter asked for silence and said in a loud voice, "Romans,[a] now let there be a just judgment between Simon and me! [23]You decide which of us, he or I, has placed his faith in the living God.[a] [24]Let Simon revive the body placed here! Then you shall trust him as the messenger of God. [25]If, however, he is unable to do it, I will call upon my God. I will return the son alive to his mother. [26]Then you shall believe this one, who has been a guest among you, is a magician and a seducer."

[27]When everyone heard these things, what Peter had said seemed just to them. [28]They exhorted Simon saying, "Now, if there is anything to you, show it openly! [29]Either put him to shame, or be put to shame. Why are you <just> standing <there>? Get on with it! Begin!"

[30]Although Simon saw all of them urging him on, he just stood <there,> silent. [31]<But> when he noticed that the people had <now> become quiet and were watching him, Simon spoke out: "Romans,[a] if you see the dead man rise, will you throw Peter out of the city?"

28:17 • *to put caps . . . the bier:* These actions indicate that the slaves were being freed in honor of their deceased master. Before agreeing to raise the senator, Peter asks for the assurance that their manumission will not be revoked.
28:20 • *the marvels of God* (*dei mirabilia*): See note on AcPetVerc 5:19.
28:29 • *standing (stas):* Perhaps a pun on the Simonian title, "Standing One" (AcPetMart 2[31]:13, 15); but for something like the complete phrase see also Acts 1:11.

28:34 ᵃCf. *Mart. Pol.* 13:1

28:38 ᵃ» 23:8

ᵇCf. Mk 9:43; Mt 3:12; Lk 3:17

28:47 ᵃ» 23:8

[32]All the people said, "We will not only throw him out, but at the same time we will burn him with fire!"

[33]Simon went up to the dead man's head. After he bowed down three times and raised himself up three times, he showed the people how the head would rise, move, open its eyes and bow to Simon. [34]Right away they began to ask for wood and firebrands in order to burn Peter with flame.[a]

[35]Peter, however, received power from Christ and raised his voice to those who were crying out against him: [36]"Now I see, people of Rome, that I may not say that you are foolish and empty so long as your eyes, your ears and your hearts are blinded. [37]How long will your perception be obscured? Don't you see that you are cheated when you think that a dead man is raised who has not gotten up? [38]It would have been enough for me, Romans,[a] to keep quiet, to die in silence, and to leave you among the illusions of this world; but I have the punishment of unquenchable fire before my eyes.[b] [39]So, if you approve, let the dead man speak! Let him raise himself, if he lives! [40]Let him free his wrapped chin with his own hands and call to his mother! [41]To you who are shouting, let him say, 'Why are you shouting?' Let him gesture to you with his hand! [42]Now, if you wish to see that he is dead and you are spellbound, let this one, who has persuaded you to withdraw from Christ, draw back from the bier! [43]Then you will see how that one remains in the same condition as when you saw him brought in."

[44]Agrippa, the prefect, could endure it no longer. He got up and pushed Simon <aside> with his own hand.

[45]Then the dead man lay again as he had been before. So the people turned away from Simon's magic in a rage. [46]They began to call out, "Listen, Caesar: If the dead man doesn't rise, let Simon be burned in place of Peter, since he really did blind us."

[47]Peter, however, extended his hand and said, "O Romans,[a] show patience now! [48]Am I telling you that Simon should be burned when the boy is revived? If I say so, you will do it!"

28:36 • *people of Rome (populi Romani):* The expression here differs from the more frequent "Romans" (see note on 23:8).
28:46 • *Listen, Caesar:* The address to Caesar is intrusive here, though the contest between Simon and Peter does take place in Nero's presence in Pseudo-Marcellus; and see 41:7.

28:33 *After he bowed down …:* The whole verse is obscure, possibly corrupt; the translation follows Bonnet and Turner.

28:51 ªCf. Mt 5:44; Lk
6:28; 2Clem 13:4

28:52 ªCf. Ac 8:22

28:53 ªCf. 1Pt 2:9

[49]The people shouted back, "Even if you don't want it, Peter, we'll do it!"

[50]Peter said to them, "If you persist in this, the boy will not rise, for we have not learned to return evil for evil. [51]We have been taught rather to love our enemies and to pray for our persecutors.[a] [52]If even he—this man—is able to repent, this is for the best;[a] for God will not remember evil deeds. [53]Let him enter the light of Christ![a] [54]Yet, if he cannot, let him possess the portion of his father, the devil! [55]Your hands, however, will not be polluted."

[56]When he had said this to the people, he approached the boy. But before he revived him he said to his mother, "Will these young men, whom you have set free in honor of your son, be able to serve their master as free men when he is alive? [57]I know that the spirit of some will be hurt when they see that your son is raised, since they will <expect to> be enslaved again. [58]Let them, rather, all remain free, receiving their provisions as before, because your son is about to be raised and they should be with him." [59]Peter observed her still longer, to see what she thought.

[60]The boy's mother said, "What else can I do? And so it is, in the presence of the prefect, I say: [61]Everything I intended to use to honor my son's body, these men shall get to keep."

[62]Peter said to her, "Let the rest be distributed to the widows!" [63]Rejoicing in his mind, Peter said in <his> spirit, "Lord, you who are merciful, Jesus Christ, appear to your Peter, who is calling upon you, just as you always have acted mercifully and bountifully. [64]In front of all these who have obtained their freedom so they can serve, let Nicostratus now arise!" [65]Then, touching the boy's side, Peter said, "Get up!"

[66]The boy got up and took off his burial cloth. He sat up, released his chin, and asked for other clothes. [67]He came down from the bier and said to Peter, "I beg you, sir, let's go to Christ, our Lord—I saw

---

28:50 • *We have not learned to return evil for evil* (*Malum enim pro malo non novimus retribuere*): See AcJohn 81:6, and note and further refs. at AcPaul 2.5:13.

28:54 • *his father, the devil* (*patris sui diaboli*): This expression or its equivalent, probably deriving from John 8:44 ("You are of your father the devil"; Vulg. *ex patre diaboli estis*), occurs elsewhere in the apocryphal acts; see, e.g., AcAndPas 21:4; 40:2; 49:3; AcThom 32:6.

28:62 • *for the rest* (*cetera*): Poupon suggests *another part*. In either case, the request is fulfilled in 29:6–7.

28:64 • *so they can serve*: The object of service is not specified. Freed slaves would remain obligated to perform service for their former masters, though service to Christ may be intended here.

him speaking with you. [68]He said to you, as he showed me to you, 'Bring him here to me, for he is mine.' "

[69]When Peter heard this from the boy, he was greatly strengthened in his mind by the Lord's help. [70]Peter said to the people, "Romans, [a] this is how the dead are revived; this is the way they converse; this is the way they walk about when they have been raised—and <this is how> they live until the time chosen by God. [71]So then, if you who have come together for the spectacle turn <now> from these evils of yours—from all of your manmade gods, and from all impurity and desire— [72]you will find communion with Christ as believers: you will obtain eternal life."

29 From that hour they worshiped him as a god and placed at his feet whoever was sick in their households so that he would heal them.[a] [2]When the prefect saw a great multitude attending to Peter, he signaled Peter that he should depart. [3]So Peter told the people to come to Marcellus's house—though the boy's mother had begged Peter to visit her house. [4]But Peter had arranged to <go to> Marcellus's on the Lord's day to see the widows, since Marcellus had promised that they would be cared for by his own hand.

[5]The boy who had arisen said, "I won't leave Peter." So his mother returned to her house joyfully—gladly.

[6]On the next day, after the Sabbath, she came to Marcellus's house bringing two thousand gold pieces for Peter. [7]She said to Peter, "Distribute these among the virgins belonging to Christ, who serve him."

[8]When the boy who had risen from the dead saw that he had not given gifts to anyone, he went home and opened his <treasure> chest. [9]He presented four thousand gold pieces, saying to Peter, "Look, I, who was restored to life, offer a double gift along with myself as a speaking sacrifice to God from this day onward."

29:1 [a]Cf. APeBG 1:2; APeVer 4:5; Ac 5:16–17

29:4 • *on the Lord's day (die dominico):* See AcPetBG 1:1 and note; AcThom 29:4.
29:9 • *speaking sacrifice (loquentem victimam):* This expression perhaps owes something to Paul's θυσίαν ζῶσαν (rsv "living sacrifice"; Vulg. hostiam viventem) in Rom 12:1. In the NT, θυσία is the only word *hostia* translates in the Vulg. (Bergren, 1991: 72b); *victima* translates both θυσία and σφάγιον (ibid., 171a).

28:72 *as believers:* Three leaves containing material from PsClemRec 4.5–10 are bound into V here; these additions were apparently inserted in the seventh century (see Vouaux, 1922: 392 n. e).

3

THE MARTYRDOM OF THE
HOLY APOSTLE PETER
(Mt. Athos [A]; Actus Vercellenses)

1 (30) On the Lord's day, Peter addressed the brothers and sisters and exhorted them to faith in Christ— [2]many senators were present, and more knights <as well as> wealthy women and matrons, being strengthened in faith.

[3]One of the women there was very wealthy. She was known as Chryse, because every vessel she possessed was golden. [4]She had used neither a silver nor a glass vessel from her birth, but only golden ones. [5]She said to Peter, "Peter, servant of God, the one you say is God came to me in a dream and said, 'Chryse, give Peter, my servant, ten thousand gold pieces, for you are indebted to him!' [6]I have brought them now, so as not to suffer harm from the one who appeared to me and <then> returned to heaven." [7]And when she had said this, she put the money down and went away.

[8]When Peter saw it, he praised the Lord because the oppressed were about to be relieved.

[9]Then some of the bystanders said to him, "Peter! Aren't you wrong to take this money from her? [10]She is accused of wantonness throughout Rome. She does not keep to one man only but goes so far as to approach her own servants. [11]Have no part in her golden table, but let her property be sent back to her!"

1:1 • *On the Lord's day* (κυριακῆς οὔσης): See note on AcPetBG 1:1.
1:3 • *Chryse* (Χρυσή, *Chrysis*), that is, "Golden One."
1:10 • *to approach her own servants:* Cf. PsClemRec 9.32; PsClemHom 14.6. Sexual relations with male slaves was considered the worst sort of depravity that a Roman woman might engage in.

The Martyrdom ...: A begins here.
1:1 *to faith in Christ* (εἰς τὴν τοῦ Χριστοῦ πίστιν): So A; V *ut persevarent in fide domini nostri Iesu Christi* ("to persevere in the faith of our Lord Jesus Christ").

1:11 *Have no part ...:* The translation follows A; V "If you approve, share with her nothing of the table of our Lord Jesus Christ, but let her fire [*ignis eius*, presumably reading τὸ πῦρ αὐτῆς for τὸ παρ' αὐτῆς, as in A] be sent to her."

[12]When Peter heard this, he laughed and said to the brothers and sisters, "Who she is with regard to the rest of her life, I do not know. [13]As for why I took the money, I did not take it without reason. [14]She brought it as Christ's debtor, and she gives it to Christ's servants, since he himself has provided for them."

2 (31) They brought the sick to him on the Sabbath, asking that he might heal them of their diseases. [2]And so, many paralytics were healed, as well as those suffering from gout and two- or four-day fevers. [3]Whoever trusted in the name of Jesus Christ was healed of every bodily disease, and many were added to the Lord's grace each day.ª

[4]After a few days, Simon the magician promised the crowd that he would convict Peter of having trusted not in a true God but in a false one. [5]Now, although Simon created many illusions, those disciples who were already firm laughed at him. [6]He made some spirits approach them in dining rooms, but these were only appearances—things that did not really exist. [7]What more is to be said? Although he had been exposed many times in his magic, he still made the ill appear well for a brief time and likewise the blind. [8]Once he made many who were dead seem to live and move—Nicostratus, for example. [9]But in all these things Peter followed Simon and exposed him in the presence of spectators. [10]Simon was constantly scorned and scoffed by the Roman crowd, and he was not believed because the things he promised to do did not come about. [11]So he finally

---

1:12 • *he laughed and said* (A γελάσας εἶπεν; V *subrisit et dixit*): See note on AcPet-Verc 6:13.

1:14 • *She brought it ...* : Poupon (1997: 1102) suggests a comparison with Commodus's mistress Marcia, who made substantial donations to the Roman church (Hippolytus *Ref.* 9.12).

2:4 • *Simon the magician* (A Σίμων ὁ μάγος): V identifies Simon simply by his name, *Simon*; but see Acts 8:9 "But there was a man named Simon who had previously practiced magic (ἀνὴρ δέ τις ὀνόματι Σίμων προϋπῆρχεν ... μαγεύων)"; 8:11 "for a long time he [Simon] had amazed them with his magic (ταῖς μαγείαις)."

2:5 • *laughed* (A κατεγέλων): See note on AcPetVerc 6:13.

2:7 • *What more is to be said?* (A καὶ τί γὰρ λέγειν; V lacks an equivalent phrase): A familiar figure of speech; cf. Heb 11:32 (καὶ τί ἔτι λέγω;); AcAndPas 61:8; Ps.-Titus 19.284; 20.386; also Polybius 9.30 1 (τίς χρεία πλείω λέγειν;); Josephus *Ant.* 20.11.1 (καὶ τί δὲ πλείω λέγειν;); 1 *Clem.* 45:6 (τί γὰρ εἴπωμεν;). Similarly, AcPetVerc 24:13 "What is more besides (*et quid plura*)?"

2:8 *Nicostratus* (V *Nicostratum*): A, placing the two elements of the name in reverse order, has Στρατόνικον ("Stratonicus"). Reference to this episode, which is not actually reported in A, suggests that the *Martyrdom* was extracted from a more extensive copy of the *Acts of Peter.*

said to them, "Romans![a] Now you think that Peter has overcome me as though he were stronger, and you pay more attention to him. [12]You are deceived: tomorrow I'll leave behind you who are thoroughly godless and impious. [13]I'll fly up to God, whose Power I am, though weakened; if now you have fallen, behold I am the Standing One. [14]I will go up to the Father and say to him, [15]"Even me, the Standing One, your son, they wished to overthrow; but, not heeding them, I returned to myself.' "

3 (32) Already on the next day a great crowd gathered at the Sacred Way to see Simon fly. [2]But Peter had seen a vision, and he came to the place to refute him again in this. [3]Simon stood in a high place, and when he saw Peter, he began to speak: [4]"Peter, now most of all, as I am about to ascend in the presence of all these onlookers, I say this to you: If your God is able, the one whom the Jews killed—and they stoned you who were chosen by him—let him show that faith in him is from God! [5]Let him show now whether it is worthy of God! [6]For my part, by ascending to him I will reveal to this whole crowd what sort of being I am." [7]And suddenly, when he was lifted into the

---

2:13 • *whose Power I am* (A οὗ ἡ δύναμις ἐγώ εἰμι; V *cuius ego virtutem*): Cf. Acts 8:10 "This man is that power of God (ἡ δύναμις τοῦ θεοῦ) which is called Great."
• *the Standing One* (also in 2:15): Cf. Hippolytus *Ref.* 6.9, 17; PsClemRec 1.72; 2.7, 11; 3.47; PsClemHom 2.22, 24; 18.6–7; Clement of Alexandria *Strom.* 2.11.52.
2:14 • *I will go up to the Father and say to him* (A καὶ ἀνέρχομαι πρὸς τὸν πατέρα καὶ ἐρῶ αὐτῷ; V *et ego vado ad patrem omnium et dico illi*): Cf. John 20:17 ἀναβαίνω πρὸς τὸν πατέρα μου ("I am ascending to my Father"; Vulg. *ascendo ad patrem meum*); Vouaux (1922: 408 n. 1) suggests that the author wishes to present Simon's flight as a caricature of Jesus' ascension.
3:4 • *they stoned you:* "You" in this verse is plural, i.e., Peter and/or his predecessors in dying for the new faith, most notably Stephen (see Acts 7:58).

2:14–15 *I will go up ... returned to myself:* V "I will fly up to the Lord, whose power I know since you have fallen from me. I am going to the Father of all, and shall say to him, 'They have injured your Son; this is why I am returning to you.' "
3:1 *the Sacred Way,* following Lipsius and Vouaux (1922: n. e). A reads ἀκρίβειαν ("punctually"); V reads *ad platea<m>*, which could refer to any major street.
3:2 *Peter had seen a vision, and he came to the place ...:* V "Peter came <there> so as to be among them." A again shows its dependence on a more complete form of the AcPet by inserting a summary of the events of AcPetVerc 4 at this point: "For when he entered Rome, he astonished the

crowds by flying. But Peter, who convicted him, was not then present in Rome— <the city> which the deceiver so disturbed with his illusions that some marveled at him."
3:3–7 *Simon stood ... looked to Peter:* V "Simon came and spoke to Peter in a loud voice: 'Look Peter, since I am about to go to God in front of these people watching me, I say to you, Peter, if the one who is your God is able, whom the Jews destroyed and stoned you [pl.] who were gathered by him, let him show what sort of faith you have; I, however, am going to him.' Suddenly he was seen in the heights by all who looked throughout the whole city above all the temples and hills."

3:18 [a]Cf. Ac 8:36; 10:47

heights, and everyone throughout all Rome saw him lifted above the city's temples and hills, the faithful looked to Peter.

[8]When Peter saw this marvelous sight, he cried out to the Lord Jesus Christ, saying, "If you allow him to do what he has undertaken, all who have believed in you will now be scandalized. [9]All the signs and wonders which you gave <them> through me will be discredited. [10]So speed your grace, Lord! Let him be deprived of power and fall down—but not be killed! [11]Rather let him become powerless, and break his leg in three places."

[12]<And> so <it was that> Simon fell down and broke his leg in three places. [13]Then they stoned him, and each one went home; and from then on they all trusted Peter.

[14]Soon one of Simon's friends came along the road. His name was Gemellus, and he had a Greek wife. [15]Simon had received many things from him. [16]On seeing that he had broken his leg, he said, "Simon, if the Power of God is utterly broken, shall not this God whose Power you are be blinded?" [17]Now even Gemellus came running to Peter and followed him, saying, "I too wish to be one of those who have faith in Christ."

[18]Peter replied, "What stands in the way now?[a] Speak, brother! Come and join us."

[19]Although Simon was in a bad state, he found some to carry him on a litter from Rome to Aricia by night. [20]After his stay there he was taken to a certain Castor in Terracina, who had been banished from Rome on a charge of magic. [21]When he was operated on there, Simon, messenger of the devil, gave up the last of his life.

3:14 • *Gemellus:* See Ficker, 1903: 56.
• *a Greek wife:* This detail, not present in V, may be a dim reflection of the association of Simon with Helen of Troy. Poupon (1997: 1105) suggests that Gemellus's wife should be understood as a disciple of Helen, who is Simon's consort in some traditions.
3:21 • *messenger of the devil* (ὁ τοῦ διαβόλου ἄγγελος; V *angelum satanae*): The phrase in Greek or Latin could contain a veiled reference to the Simonian title, "Angel of God." Vouaux (1922: 415 n. 6) rightly compares 2 Cor 12:7 "a messenger of Satan" (ἄγγελος σατανᾶ [note v.ll.]; Vulg. *angelus Satanae*). cf. AcPetVerc 17:56; 18:3.

3:11–13 *Rather let him become … trusted Peter:* V "'So quickly, Lord, make your grace and show your power to all who are watching me. But I pray not that he should die, but that he should be confused in his limbs.' And right away he [Simon] fell to the ground, and broke his leg in three places. Then all the faithful stoned him, and gave praise to God."

3:16 *if the Power … be blinded:* V "Are you the Power of God? Who has broken your leg? Is it not God himself, whose Power you say you are?"

3:21 *When he was operated on there:* V "There two doctors operated on him."

4:1 ᵃCf. APeBG 2:7

4 (33) Meanwhile Peter remained in Rome rejoicing in the Lord along with the brothers and sisters, and giving thanks day and night[a] for the crowd who were being led to the holy name of the Lord's grace daily. ²The concubines of the prefect Agrippa also came to Peter. There were four of them: Agrippina, Nikaria, Euphemia, and Doris. ³When they heard the message concerning purity and all the words of the Lord, their souls were smitten. ⁴Because they agreed together to remain pure, apart from Agrippa's bed, they were troubled by him. ⁵Agrippa was at a loss and grieving over them because he loved them <so> greatly that he was watching them and sent a spy <to find out> where they were going. ⁶He learned it was to Peter. So when they came <back>, he told them, "That Christian taught you to have no relations with me. ⁷Know that I will both destroy you and burn him alive!"

⁸Then <and there> they resolved to endure every evil from Agrippa rather than be stirred by passion any longer, for they were strengthened by the power of Jesus.

5 (34) Now there was a very beautiful woman who was the wife of Albinus, a friend of Caesar; her name was Xanthippe. ²She, too, came to Peter with the other matrons, and she withdrew from <relations with> Albinus.

4:2 • *four of them …:* V omits the number and names; in the other versions the names vary (see Vouaux, 1922: 417 n. j).

4:3 • *the message concerning purity …:* This phrase is reminiscent of (or is perhaps the inspiration for) AcPaulThec 7:1.

5:1 • *a friend of Caesar:* τοῦ Καίσαρος φίλου (V *viri amici Caesaris*), a phrase possibly with a technical connotation; cf. John 19:12.

• *Agrippa:* If Agrippa is imagined to be an urban prefect, he will have the authority to punish disturbances of public order. Citizens might appeal to the emperor, but as a provincial, Peter would have had no such recourse. No urban prefect by this name is known; the name may be intended to create a link to king Herod Agrippa, familiar from Acts 25–26.

4:1 *Meanwhile …:* The Patmos Manuscript (P) and most other versions of the *Martyrdom* start at this point, although the opening words vary.

were being led …: V "coming to belief in the name of Christ"; cf. Acts 2:47; 4:12.

4:3–8 *When they heard …:* V "Hearing that they ought to observe the greatest purity, and agreeing among themselves, they abstained from sleeping with Agrippa the prefect. Although he harassed them, they made excuses and refused to go near him. He viewed them with anger thereafter; he <even> sent a spy to them, so as to know where

they went—and learned that they went to Peter. Agrippa said to them, 'Peter is the one who has forbidden you to have relations with me; he is the one who taught you this. Know, then, that both you and he will perish.' But they were prepared to suffer every evil he might commit against them, because the Lord strengthened them."

5:1 *Albinus:* V "an illustrious man."

5:2 *she withdrew from …:* V "she suffered from her husband because she kept her chastity. Now he kept her chastity."

6:1–4 ªCf. *Mart. Pol.* 5:1

6:2–3 ªCf. APeVer 1:4

[3]He became furious <about this>, since he loved Xanthippe and was amazed that she would not even sleep in the same bed with him. [4]He raged like a beast, wishing to lay hands on Peter—he knew him to have been the cause of her departure from his bed. [5]Many other women, too, had withdrawn from their husbands when they fell in love with the teaching about purity. [6]Even men kept themselves from the beds of their own wives because they wished to worship God piously and purely.

[7]There was a great disturbance in Rome, and Albinus informed Agrippa of his concerns, saying to him, [8]"Either avenge me against Peter, who caused my wife's separation from me, or I will avenge myself."

[9]Agrippa replied that he, too, had suffered similar things from him, saying, "He made my concubines separate from me."

[10]So Albinus said to him, "What are you waiting for, Agrippa? [11]Let's find him and destroy him as a meddler: then we'll have our wives <back> and also avenge those whose wives he has separated from them but who couldn't have destroyed him <on their own>."

6 (35) While they were planning these things, ª Xanthippe learned of her husband's conspiracy with Agrippa. [2]She sent to Peter and told him that he should leave Rome. The rest of the brothers and sisters, along with Marcellus, <also> asked him to depart. [3]But Peter said to them, "Shall we run away, brothers and sisters?"ª

5:3 • *He became furious:* Cf. Justin *2 Apol.* 2.
5:11 • *as a meddler* (ὡς περίεργον ἄνδρα): Noting that A reads ὡς μάγον ("as a magician"), Vouaux (1922: 423 n. 2) suggests that here Peter's "meddling" is considered by his opponents to be "magic"; cf. Acts 19:19 ἱκανοὶ δὲ τῶν τὰ περίεργα πραξάντων (RSV "And a number of those who practiced magic arts . . .").

5:4 *wishing to lay hands on Peter . . . :* V "seeking a way to destroy Peter."
5:5–6 *Many other women . . . purely:* V "Thus several other honorable women withdrew from their husbands, when they heard the preaching concerning chastity. Men also separated from their wives because they wished to serve God chastely and purely"; cf. AcPaul 7:1.
5:7–11 *There was a great disturbance . . . :* V "When no little stir had been aroused by Albinus, he reported to the prefect concerning his wife. He said to him, 'Either you defend me from Peter, who has persuaded her to become a Christian, or I will vindicate myself.' Then the prefect answered Albinus, 'I have suffered the same.' Albinus said

to the prefect, 'So what are you doing? Why don't you defend yourself and everyone <else>? Let's kill him, so that we may <again> take possession of our wives.'" Cf. Acts 19:19 (see note on 5:11 below); AcPaulThec 14:1; 15:2–3; 16:1; AcAndPas 1:3.
6:1–2 *While they were planning these things . . . :* V "There was a gathering at Xanthippe's house. She reported to Peter <what was going on>, and begged him to leave Rome, so that he would not have a place in the evil hour. And all the brothers said to him . . ." A leaf has fallen out of V at this point; V resumes at 7:12. The versions of the *Martyrdom* show great variety in the opening lines; see Vouaux, 1922: 422–24.

⁴They answered, "No, but <you must,> so that you will still be able to serve the Lord."

⁵Having been persuaded by the brothers and sisters, he departed alone, saying, "Let none of you leave with me! ⁶Rather, I'll go alone, after I have changed my appearance."

⁷As he went out through the gate, he saw the Lord coming into Rome. ⁸<And as soon> as he noticed him he said, "Lord, why are you here?"

⁹The Lord said to him, "I am going into Rome to be crucified."

¹⁰Peter said to him, "Lord, are you to be crucified again?"

¹¹He said to him, "Yes, Peter, I am to be crucified again."

¹²When Peter came to himself and saw the Lord returning to heaven, he himself turned back to Rome, rejoicing and glorifying the Lord because he himself had said to him, "I am to be crucified"— ¹³this was going to happen to Peter.

7 (36) When he came back up to the brothers and sisters and told them what he had seen, they mourned in <their> souls. ²They lamented and said, "We ask you, Peter, take thought for us who are younger!"

³Peter told them <this>: "If it is the Lord's wish, it will happen, even if we do not want it. ⁴Yet the Lord is able to strengthen you in faith in him. ⁵He will establish you in himself and cause you, whom he planted, to grow in him, so that you too can plant others through him.ª ⁶As long as the Lord wishes me to be in the flesh, I'll not object; but when he wishes to take me, I'll rejoice and be glad."

⁷As Peter said these things, and all the brothers and sisters lamented, four soldiers, arrested him and took him to Agrippa, who, because of his sickness, commanded that he be crucified on the charge of godlessness.

6:10 • *to be crucified again?* (πάλιν σταυροῦσαι;): Cf. AcPaul 4.1:11 (PHeid 7).
6:12 • *When Peter came to himself* (καὶ ἐλθὼν εἰς ἑαυτὸν ὁ Πέτρος) …: Vouaux (1922: 428 n. 1) identifies as the "probable" origin of this tradition John 21:18–19 ("When you were young, … ; but when you are old …") and 2 Pet 1:14 ("I know that the putting off of my body will be soon").

6:4 *<you must,> so that … the Lord:* S "remain in the flesh for our sake" (cf. Phil 1:24 τὸ δὲ ἐπιμένειν ἐν σαρκὶ ἀναγκαιότερον δι' ὑμᾶς); the discussion is greatly extended in L.
6:7 *"Lord, why are you here?"* (Κύριε, ποῦ ὧδε;): L expands the scene, and renders the phrase in the famous question, *Domine, quo vadis?* (= John 13:36; 16:5 Vulg., translating κύριε, ποῦ ὑπάγεις).
6:9 *to be crucified:* L adds *iterum* ("again").
7:7 *four soldiers* (στρατιῶται τέσσαρες): P

ἱεροπολῖται τεσσάρεις, the rare noun presumably here to be rendered "four *citizens* [or: *members*] *of the holy place*"; cf. θεοὶ πολῖται quoted in LSJ, s.v. πολίτης II. (p. 1435a). See also Poupon, 1997: 1109 n. b.

to Agrippa: Some of the versions add ten servants, and/or a priest, to the arresting party; details in Vouaux, 1922: 430 n. f.

on the charge of godlessness: L adds a lengthy discussion between Peter and the prefect.

[8]Now the whole crowd of brothers and sisters ran together—both rich and poor, orphans and widows, strong and weak—wishing to see Peter, and to snatch him away. [9]Meanwhile, the people called out incessantly, with a single voice, "What injustice has Peter done, Agrippa? What evil has he done to you? [10]Tell the Romans, lest this man die and the Lord destroy us!"

7:11 ªCf. 2Tm 2:3
7:14 ªCf. Jn 8:44

[11]When Peter arrived at the place and quieted the crowd, he said, "You who are soldiers for Christ,[a] you who hope on Christ: remember the signs and wonders which you saw done through me! [12]Remember God's compassion toward you—how many healings he has accomplished for you. [13]Wait for him who will come and reward each one according to their actions. [14]Now, don't be bitter toward Agrippa; he is a servant of his father's activity.[a] [15]Besides, this will come about in any case, for the Lord has shown me what is to happen. [16]But why do I delay, and not approach the cross?"

8 (37) When he approached the cross and stood by it, he began to speak:

[2]O name of the cross, hidden mystery!
O inexpressible grace that is spoken in the name of the
cross!
[3]O human nature, that cannot be separated from God!
O unspeakable and inseparable love,
that cannot be made known through unclean lips!
[4]I seize you now at the end, as I begin my release from here;
I shall reveal what you are!
[5]I shall not restrain that which has been shut up within my soul
for a long time,
namely, the hidden mystery of the cross.

[6]"You who hope on Christ do not consider this visible thing the cross, for there is something other than this visible one. [7]Now, most of all, since you who are able to hear can hear from me as I begin the last and final hour of my life, listen! [8]Separate your souls from

---

7:8 • *and to snatch him away:* Cf. AcAndPas 52:4; AcPaul 5.2:15; AcThom 165:1.

7:10 *Tell the Romans ... destroy us:* C "We must fear, lest this man die and his Lord destroy us all"; cf. AcPaulThec 27:2; 32:1–3; 36:2; AcPaulMar 3:11–12.
7:12 *... he has accomplished for you:* V resumes at this point.
7:14 *of his father's activity:* V adds "and his tradition"; cf. Matt 16:27; Rom 2:6.
7:16 *But why do I delay, and not approach the cross:* L greatly expands Peter's speech, and localizes the

cross "at the place called the Naumachia, near the obelisk of Nero on the hill" (i.e., on the Vatican hill); V "But why do I hesitate and not proceed to the cross?" Peter's speech is abbreviated in various ways in many of the witnesses; see Vouaux, 1922: 434–36.
8:6 *this visible one:* P adds "in accordance with Christ's passion" (κατὰ τὸ τοῦ χριστοῦ πάθος); cf. AcAndPas 1:14.

8:12 [a]Cf. PsTiEp
27.404

9:4–7 [a]Cf. APeVer
8:18

9:8 [a]Cf. 1Cor 2:7

everything belonging to the senses—from everything that <mere-
ly> appears and does not truly exist! [9]Blind this sight of yours; block
this hearing of yours, which are actions in the realm of appearance;
and you will come to know what happened concerning Christ and
the whole mystery of your salvation. [10]It is the hour for you, Peter,
to hand your body over to those who will receive it. [11]Take it, then,
you for whom it is fitting. [12]I ask you, public executioners, to cru-
cify me <with my> head down[a] — no other way. [13]I'll explain why to
those who will listen."

9 (38) When they had hung him up in the manner he had request-
ed, he began to speak again: [2]"You for whom it is fitting to hear, pay
special attention to what I am about to tell you now as I am hanging. [3]Understand the mystery of all nature and what the beginning
of all things was. [4]For the first human being, whose race I bear in
appearance, fell head downward and thereby displayed a process of
generation that had not existed before: it was dead because it had
no movement. [5]When this one, who also cast his own beginning
onto the earth, was pulled down, he established the whole cosmic
order, and this is why: [6]he was suspended as an image in which he
displayed the things on the right as on the left and those on the left
as on the right. [7]He changed all the signs of their nature <into their
opposites>, so that he considered beautiful the things that are not
beautiful, and good the things that are in reality bad.[a]

[8]"It was concerning this that the Lord, in a mystery,[a] said <this>:
'Unless you make the things on the right as the things on the left
and the things on the left as the things on the right, the things
above as the things below, and the things behind as the things in
front, you will not recognize the kingdom.'

8:9 • *Blind this sight of yours ...:* Those who are able to understand are invited to
maim (πηρώσατε) themselves, presumably in a metaphorical sense.
9:4 • *the first human being ...:* Poupon (1997: 1111 n. A) suggests that a Hermetic
myth stands behind this section rather than Genesis.
9:8 • *Unless you make ...:* Cf. 2 Clem. 12:2; Thom (NHC II,2) 22: 37,25–35; AcThom
92:1; Acts Phil. 140.

8:9 *the whole mystery of your salvation:* P adds
"and let these things be spoken to you, who hear
<them> as things not spoken."
9:3 *the beginning of all things was:* P adds here 1 Cor
15:47 "For the first human being was from the
earth, of dust; but the second human being was
from heaven."
9:6 *as an image:* A adds "of a calling." The rest of

the paragraph is misunderstood in V.
9:7 *that are in reality bad:* The next two sentences
are included from V; they are lacking in A.
9:8 *will not recognize* (οὐ μὴ ἐπιγνῶτε): V "will not
enter."

    kingdom: V adds "of heaven"; L S R add "of
God"; see note on AcPetVerc 7:21.

[9] "This understanding I now set before you, and the manner in which you see me hanging is a representation of that human being who first departed into the realm of generation. [10] Now, my beloved ones, you—you who now hear and you who will soon hear—you ought to desist from your former error[a] and return. [11] For it is fitting to mount the cross of Christ, who is the word stretched out, the one and only, concerning whom the Spirit said, 'What is the Christ but the word, the sound of God?'

[12] "So it is that the word is the upright tree on which I am crucified: [13] The sound is the crosspiece, human nature; but the nail that attaches the crosspiece on the upright tree at the middle is human conversion and repentance.

10

(39) "Because you have revealed these things and made them known to me, O Word of life, now called tree by me, I thank you. [2] Not with these lips which are nailed up, nor by the tongue through which truth and falsehood proceed. [3] Rather I thank you, King, with this voice that is apprehended through silence—that is not heard openly, that does not proceed through the organs of the body, that does not enter ears of flesh,[a] [4] that is not heard by corruptible substance, that is neither subsisting in the cosmos and poured forth in the earth, [5] nor is it written in books, nor does it belong to one person while not belonging to another. [6] Rather, I thank you, Jesus Christ, by this your voice, by which the spirit within me encounters you as it loves you, speaks with you, and sees you. [7] You are perceptible only to the spirit;[a] you who are father to me; you who are mother to me; you who are brother to me; you, friend; you, servant; you, steward. [8] You are the all, and the all is in you.[a] [9] You are what is, and there is nothing else that is except you alone.[a]

[10] "Now, brothers and sisters, when you too take refuge in this one and learn that you exist in him alone, you shall obtain these things concerning which he <describes> to you as [11] 'things which neither the eye has seen nor the ear heard nor has it entered the human heart.'[a]

9:10 [a]» AcPeVer 2:10
10:3 [a]» APeBG 2:17
10:11 [a]Cf. 1Cor 2:11
10:7 [a]Cf. 1Cor 2:9; Th (NHC II,2) 17: 36,5–9
10:8 [a]Cf. Th (NHC II,2) 77: 46,25–27

9:11 • ... *the word, the sound of God* (ὁ λόγος, ἦχος τοῦ θεοῦ): If this is a quotation, its origin is unknown; but cf. Ignatius *Magn.* 8:2

9:11 *to mount the cross of Christ:* A omits the rest of the chapter.
　　What is the Christ...? Poupon (1997: 1112 n. C) emends "Christ," which is in the mss, to "Cross," judging that the abbreviated forms (nomina sacra) might easily be confused.

9:13 *the nail* (ἦλος): P S λόγον ("the word").
10:2 *truth and lies come out:* Perhaps an echo of Jas 3:5–10. A adds "nor by this word proceeding by the skill belonging to human nature"; P "silence of voice."
10:6 *this your voice:* P "silence of voice."

11:6 ªCf. Mt 8:22;
Lk 9:60

¹²We ask now about the things that you promised to give us, immaculate Jesus;

We praise you, and we thank you.
¹³We who are still weak human beings glorify you,

and we confess that you alone are God and no other,

to whom be glory both now and to the end of all the ages, Amen!

11 (40) The multitude standing there pronounced the "Amen" with a great resounding noise. ²Together with that "Amen," Peter gave his spirit over to the Lord. ³When Marcellus saw that blessed Peter had breathed his last, he took him down from the cross with his own hands, without receiving authorization from anyone—this was not allowed. ⁴He washed <him> in milk and wine, and, having ground together seven minas of myrrh and fifty <minas> of aloe and other herbs, he embalmed his remains. ⁵He filled a stone sarcophagus with Attic honey of the greatest value and placed them in his own tomb.

⁶Peter came to Marcellus at night and said, "Marcellus, have you not heard the saying of the Lord, 'Leave the dead to be buried by their own dead'?"ª

⁷When Marcellus answered, "Yes," Peter said to him, "These things that you have provided for the dead, you have lost; for you, even while you remain alive, care for the dead as though <you yourself were> dead."

⁸When Marcellus woke up, he reported Peter's appearance to the brothers and sisters. ⁹He remained with those who had been strengthened in faith in Christ by Peter. ¹⁰He himself was further strengthened until Paul's arrival in Rome.

12 (41) Later, when Nero learned that Peter had departed from <this> life, he reproached the prefect Agrippa because Peter had

11:4 • *he embalmed his remains:* The details of the embalming material vary greatly in the manuscripts. See Vouaux, 1922: 460 n. a.
11:6 • *came to Marcellus at night:* Cf. AcPaulMart 6:2; 7:1; AcPhil 42.
12:1 • *when Nero…:* The sudden appearance of Nero has led some to suspect that the final chapter is a later addition to the document, along with AcPetVerc 1–3.

11:5 *sarcophagus,* following V, which is surely correct in understanding the "bath tub" (μάκτραν) of P thus; for μάκτρα as "sarcophagus," see the references in LSJ, s.v. 1074a–b.
11:10 *He himself was further strengthened…:* V omits this sentence. Likewise, L does not mention Paul's return to Rome, though the event appears in varying forms in all other versions (see Vouaux, 1922: 462 n. d); S even inserts a section of AcPaul 11 (the *Martyrdom*) at this point.

been killed without his permission. [2]He had wanted to punish him more severely, and to exact greater vengeance, because Peter had caused some of his close companions to separate from him by making them disciples.[a] [3]<Nero> remained so angry that for a long time he would not even speak to Agrippa, and he sought to destroy all of the brothers and sisters who had been made disciples by Peter.[a]

[4]<But> one night he saw someone scourging him and saying this:[a] "Nero, you cannot persecute or destroy the servants of Christ. Keep your hands off them!"

[5]Nero became very frightened as a result of this vision, and he left the disciples alone at that time, when Peter also departed from life. [6]Thereafter, the brothers and sisters continued rejoicing in unison and delighting in the Lord, glorifying the God and savior of our Lord Jesus Christ, together with the Holy Spirit, to whom be glory forever and ever. Amen.

12:2 [a]Cf. Phil 4:22; APaMar 1:3, 14

12:3 [a]Cf. APaMar 2:12

12:4 [a]Cf. APaMar 3:10–12; PsClR 10.61, 66; PsClH 20.19

12:4 *Keep your hands off them!* Turner: "If you do not, you will find out whether you have despised me."
12:6 *the God …:* Vouaux (1922: 466 n. b) "God and the savior, our Lord Jesus Christ, together with the Holy Spirit"; S "the Father, and the Son, and the Holy Spirit." Poupon (1997: 114 n. G) emends "Savior" to "Father," judging that the *nomina sacra* have been confused. For God (rather than Jesus Christ) as "savior" in Christian texts, see, e.g., 1 Tim 1:1; 2:3; Tit 1:3; 2:10 (cf. esp. 2:13); 3:4; Jude 25.

forever and ever. Amen. V adds the colophon, "Peace to all of the brothers, both those who read and those who listen. The Acts of Peter the Apostle and are ended in peace and Simon [sic]. Amen." The question is whether "and Simon" is a correction of the title or an extension of the wish for peace even to Simon. Unfortunately, this part of the manuscript is nearly illegible. A second explicit for the whole manuscript follows; see Baldwin, 2005: 168–70.

BIBLIOGRAPHY

TEXTS AND TRANSLATIONS

Achelis, Hans, *Acta SS. Nerei et Achillei: Texte und Untersuchung* (Texte und Untersuchungen zur Geschichte der altchristlichen Literatur 11/2; Leipzig: J. C. Hinrichs, 1893).

Allberry, C. R. C., ed., with a contribution from Hugo Ibscher, *A Manichaean Psalm-Book* (Manichaean Manuscripts in the Chester Beatty Collections 2/2; Stuttgart: Kohlhammer, 1938).

Amsler, Frédéric, François Bovon, and Bertrand Bouvier, trans., *Actes de l'apôtre Philippe: Introduction, traduction et notes* (Apocryphes: Collection de Poche de l'AELAC 8; Turnhout: Brepols, 1996).

Bedjan, Paul, *Acta martyrum et sanctorum Syriace* (7 vols.; Paris / Leipzig: A. Harrassowitz, 1890; reprinted Hildesheim: G. Olms, 1968) 1. 1–33.

Brashler, James, and Douglas M. Parrott, "The Act of Peter," in Douglas M. Parrott, ed., *Nag Hammadi Codicies V, 2–5 and VI with Papyrus Berolinensis 8502,1 and 4* (Nag Hammadi Studies 11; Coptic Gnostic Library; Leiden: Brill, 1979) 473–93.

Budge, E. A. W., "The History of Saint Peter at Rome," "The Martyrdom of Saint Peter at Rome," "Of How Saint Peter Preached in the City of Rome," and "Of How Peter Returned to the City of Rome and Put an End to Simon Magus," in idem, *The Contending of the Apostles (Maṣḥafa Gadla Ḥawâryât)* (2 vols.; London: Oxford University Press, 1899–1902; English trans. rev., 1935; reprinted Amsterdam: Philo, 1976) 1. 7–36, 37–49, 416–21, 425–33 (Ethiopic text); 2. 5–34, 417–21, 425–32 (English translation).

Cambe, Michel, *Kerygma Petri: Textus et Commentarius* (Corpus Christianorum Series Apocryphorum 15; Turnhout: Brepols, 2003).

De Bruyne, Domitien, "Deux citations apocryphes de l'apôtre Pierre," *Journal of Theological Studies* 34 (1933) 395–97.

———, "Epistula Titi, discipuli Pauli, de dispositione sanctimonii," *Revue bénédictine de critique, d'histoire et de littérature religieuses* 37 (1925) 47–72.

———, "Nouveaux fragments des Actes de Pierre, de Paul, de Jean, d'André, et de l'Apocalypse d'Élie," *Revue bénédictine de critique, d'histoire et de littérature religieuses* 25 (1908) 149–60; esp. 151–53.

Elliott, J. Keith, "The Acts of Peter," in idem, *The Apocryphal New Testament: A Collection of Apocryphal Christian Literature in an English Translation* (Oxford: Clarendon, 1993) 390–430. Based on M. R. James, *Apocryphal New Testament* (see below), but the text is newly translated.

Erbetta, Mario, ed. and trans., "Gli Atti di Pietro," in idem, *Gli apocrifi del Nuovo Testamento* (3 vols. in 4 parts; Turin: Marietti, 1966–81; 2d ed., 1975–82; reprinted 1992) 2. 135–210.

Goodspeed, Edgar J. ed., *Die ältesten Apologeten: Texte mit kurzen Einleitungen* (Göttingen: Vandenhoeck & Ruprecht, 1914; reprinted 1984).

Grenfell, B. P., and A. S. Hunt, *Oxyrhynchus Papyri, Part VI [Nos. 845-1006]* (London: Egypt Exploration Fund, 1908) 6–12.

Hennecke, Edgar, ed., *Neutestamentliche Apokryphen in Verbindung mit Fachgelehrten in deutscher Übersetzung und mit Einleitungen* (Tübingen/Leipzig: Mohr-Siebeck, 1904). Acts of Peter: introduction and translation by Gerhard Ficker 383–423.

In subsequent editions:

2d German ed., 1924; Acts of Peter (Actus Vercellenses)—introduction and translation by Ficker: 226–49;

3d German ed., 1959–64 (2 vols.; ed. with Wilhelm Schneemelcher); Acts of Peter—introduction and translation by Wilhelm Schneemelcher: 2. 177–221;

English translation of the 3d ed.: Edgar Hennecke and Wilhelm Schneemelcher, eds., R. McL. Wilson, trans. ed., *New Testament Apocrypha* (2 vols.; London: Lutterworth; Philadelphia: Westminster, 1962–65): 2. 259–322;

4th German ed., 1968–71 = a corrected reprint of the 3d ed. (no corresponding English translation published);

5th ed., 1987–89 (ed. by Schneemelcher); *Acts of Peter*—introduction and translation by Schneemelcher: 2. 243–89;

English translation of the 5th ed.: Wilhelm Schneemelcher, ed., R. McL. Wilson, trans. ed. (rev. ed.; Cambridge: Clark; Louisville: Westminster/John Knox, 1991–1992): 2. 271–321;

6th German ed., 1990–91 = a corrected reprint of the 5th ed. (no corresponding English translation published).

James, Montague Rhodes, *Apocrypha anecdota* (Texts and Studies 2.3; Cambridge: University Press, 1893).

———, *The Apocryphal New Testament: Being the Apocryphal Gospels, Acts, Epistles, and Apocalypses* (Oxford: Clarendon, 1924; 2d corrected and augmented ed. 1953; often reprinted). For more than half a century this was the standard English translation. "The Acts of Peter," 300–336.

Jolivet, Régis, and Maurice Jourjon, *Six traités anti-manichéens* (Bibliothèque augustinienne ; Œvres de saint Augustin 17; Bruges: Desclée de Brouwer, 1961).

Junod, Eric, and Jean-Daniel Kaestli, *Acta Iohannis* (Corpus Christianorum Series Apocryphorum 2; Turnhout: Brepols, 1983).

LeLoir, Louis, "Martyre de Pierre (BHO 933)," in idem, *Écrits apocryphes sur les apôtres: Traduction de l'édition arménienne de Venise*, vol . 1: *Pierre, Paul, André, Jacques, Jean* (Corpus Christianorum Series Apocryphorum 3; Turnhout: Brepols, 1986) 64–76.

Lewis, Agnes Smith, *Acta Mythologica Apostolorum Transcribed from an Arabic MS in the Convent of Deyr-es-Suriani, Egypt, and from MSS in the Convent of St. Catherine, on Mount Sinai: With Two Legends from a Vatican MS by Ignazio Guidi, and an Appendix of Palimpsest Syriac Fragments of the Acts of Judas Thomas from Cod. Sin. Syr. 30* (Horae semiticae 3; London: Clay, 1904).

Lipsius, Richard Adelbert, ed., "Actus Petri cum Simone [*Actus Vercellenses*]," and "Μαρτύριον τοῦ ἁγίου ἀποστόλου Πέτρου [Martyrdom of the Holy Apostle Peter]," in idem and Max Bonnet, eds., *Acta apostolorum apocrypha* (2 vols. in 3 parts; Leipzig: Mendelssohn,

1891–1903; reprinted Hildesheim: Georg Olms, 1959; also reprinted 1972) 1. 45–103. The standard critical edition along with that of Vouaux below. A new edition, in preparation by Gérard Poupon, is anticipated in the Brepols Corpus Christianorum Series Apocryphorum.

Michaelis, Wilhelm, "Petrus-Akten," in idem, *Die apokryphen Schriften zum Neuen Testament* (4th ed.; Sammlung Dieterich 129; Bremen: Carl Schünemann Verlag, 1964) 317–79.

Moraldi, Luigi, ed. and trans., "Atti di San Pietro," in idem, *Apocrifi del Nuovo Testamento* (2 vols.; Classici delle religioni [24], Sezione 5: Le altre confessioni cristiane; Classici UTET; Turin: Unione Tipografico-Editrice Torinese, 1971; and reprinted) 2. 963–1040.

Müller, F. W. K., *Sogdhdische Texte II* (SPAW-PHK; Berlin: Akademie-Verlag, 1934).

Nissen, Theodor Karl Johannes, ed., *S. Abercii vita* (Bibliotheca scriptorum Graecorum et Romanorum Teubneriana; Leipzig: Teubner, 1912).

Pick, Bernhard, trans., "The Acts of Peter," in idem, *The Apocryphal Acts of Peter, Paul, John, Andrew, and Thomas* (Chicago: Open Court, 1909; reprinted Eugene, Or.: Wipf & Stock, 2006) 50–122.

Poupon, Gérard, ed. and trans., "Actes de Pierre," in François Bovon, Pierre Geoltrain, and Jean-Daniel Kaestli, eds., *Écrits apocryphes chrétiens* (2 vols.; Bibliothèque de la Pléiade 442, 516; Paris: Gallimard, 1997–2005) 1. 1041–114.

Prieur, Jean-Marc, *Acta Andreae* (2 vols.; Corpus Christianorum, Series Apocryphorum 5–6. Turnout: Brepols, 1989).

Rouleau, Donald, *L'Épître apocryphe de Jacques (NH I,2)*; and Roy, Louise, *L'acte de Pierre (BG 4)* (Bibliothèque copte de Nag Hammadi Section Textes 18; Québec: Les Presses de l'Université Laval, 1987).

Sáenz, Antonio Piñero, and Gonzalo del Cerro, eds. and trans., "Hechos de Pedro," in idem, *Hechos apócrifos de los Apóstoles* (2 vols.; Madrid: Biblioteca de autores cristianos, 2004–2005) 1. 485–682.

Schenke, Hans-Martin, Hans-Gebhard, and Ursula Ulrike Kaiser, eds., *Nag Hammadi Deutsch*, vol. 2: *NHC V,2–XIII,1, BG 1 und 4* (Koptisch-gnostische Schriften 3; Griechischen christlichen Schriftsteller der ersten Jahrhunderte, neue Folge 12; Berlin / New York : de Gruyter, 2001).

Schmidt, Carl, *Die alten Petrusakten im Zusammenhang der apokryphen Apostellitteratur, nebst einem neuentdeckten Fragment* (Texte und Untersuchungen 24/1, neue Folge 9; Leipzig: Hinrichs, 1903).

Schneemelcher, Wilhelm, "Petrusakten," "The Acts of Peter," see above, Hennecke, ed., *Neutestamentliche Apokryphen.*

Tardieu, Michel, *Écrits gnostiques,* vol. 1: *Évangile selon Marie, Livre des secrets de Jean, Sagesse de Jésus et Eugnoste, Sagesse de Jésus, Acte de Pierre* (Sources gnostiques et manichéennes 1; Paris: Les Éditions du Cerf, 1984). Text 217–22; commentary 403–10.

Till, Walter C. and Hans-Martin Schenke, *Die gnostischen Schriften des koptischen Papyrus Berolinensis 8502* (2d ed.; Texte und Untersuchungen zur Geschichte der altchristlichen Literatur 60; Berlin: Akademie, 1973) 296–319.

Vetter, P., "Die armenischen apokryphen Apostelakten," *Oriens christianus* 1 (1901) 217–39.

Vouaux, Léon, *Les actes de Pierre: Introduction, textes, traduction et commentaire* (Les apocryphes du Nouveau Testament; Documents pour servir à l'étude des origines chrétiennes; Paris: Letouzey et Ané, 1922).

STUDIES AND OTHER
WORKS CITED

Adamik, Tamás, "The Language and Style of the *Acts of Peter*," in Benjamin Garcia-Herna-
dez, *Estudios de Lingüística Latina: Actas del IX coloquio Internacional de Lingüística Latina,
Universidad Autonóma de Madrid, 14–18 abril de 1997* (Bibliotheca linguae latinae; Madrid:
Ediciones Clásicas, 1998) 106–72.

Achtemeier, Paul J., "Jesus and the Disciples as Miracle Workers in the Apocryphal New
Testament," in Elizabeth Schüssler Fiorenza, ed., *Aspects of Religious Propaganda in Judaism and Early Christianity* (Notre Dame, Ind.: University of Notre Dame Press, 1976)
149–86.

Amann, Emile, "Les actes de Pierre," *DBSup* 1: 496–501.

Aune, David, "Greco-Roman Biography," in idem, ed., *Greco-Roman Literature and the New Testament: Selected Forms and Genres* (SBL Sources for Biblical Study 21; Atlanta: Scholars
Press, 1988) 107–26.

Baldwin, Matthew C., *Whose Acts of Peter? Text and Historical Context of the Actus Vercellenses*
(Wissenschaftliche Untersuchungen zum Neuen Testament 2/196; Tübingen: Mohr-
Siebeck, 2005).

Barnikol, Ernst, "Die Ertragung des Paulus in die Grundschrift der Petrusakten," *Theologishe
Jahrbücher* 2 (1934) 153–57.

———, "Marcellus in den Petrus-Akten (U und V)," *Theologishe Jahrbücher* 2 (1934) 158–64.

———, "Petrus vor dem Caesar? Ist der Praefekt in den Petrusakten ursprünglich der Caesar?" *Theologishe Jahrbücher* 2 (1934) 115–22.

———, "Spanienreise und Römerbrief des Paulus in den Petrus-Akten," *Theologishe Jahrbücher* 2 (1934) 1–12.

———, "Die Urgestalt der Petrusakten: Actus Petri cum Simone," *Theologishe Jahrbücher* 2
(1934) 165–69.

Bauckham, Richard J., "The Martyrdom of Peter in Early Christian Literature," in Hildegard
Temporini and Wolfgang Haase, eds., *Aufstieg und Niedergang der römischen Welt* 2:26.1
(Leiden: Brill1992) 539–95.

Baumstark, Anton, *Die Petrus- und Paulusacten in der litterarischen Überlieferung der syrischen
Kirche: Festgruss dem Priestercollegium des Deutschen Campo Santo zu Rom zur Feier seines 25
jährigen Bestehens (8 December 1901)* (Leipzig: Harrassowitz, 1902).

Bergmeier, Roland, "Die Gestalt des Simon Magus in Act 8 und in der simonianischen Gnosis—Aporien einer Gesamtdarstellung," *Zeitschrift für die neutestamentliche Wissenschaft*
77 (1986) 267–75.

Blumenthal, Martin, *Formen und Motive in den apokryphen Apostelgeschichten* (Texte und Untersuchungen zur Geschichte der altchristlichen Literatur 48/1; Leipzig: Hinrichs,
1933).

Bovon, François, "Miracles, magie et guérison dans les actes apocryphes des apôtres," *Journal of Early Christian Studies* 3 (1995) 245–59.

———, "The Synoptic Gospels and the Noncanonical Acts of the Apostles," *Harvard Theological Review* 81 (1988) 19–36.

———, "La vie des apôtres: traditions bibliques et narrations apocryphe," in idem, *Les actes
apocryphes des apôtres*, 141–58.

Bovon, François et al., eds., *Les actes apocryphes des apôtres: Christianisme et monde païen* (Publications de la Faculté de théologie de l'Université de Genève N° 4; Geneva: Labor et Fides, 1981).

Bovon, François, Ann Graham Brock, and Christopher R. Matthews, eds., *The Apocryphal Acts of the Apostles: Harvard Divinity School Studies* (Religions of the World; Cambridge, Mass.: Harvard University Press / Harvard University Center for the Study of World Religions, 1999).

Bovon, François, and Bertrand Bouvier, "Un fragment grec inédit des Actes de Pierre?" *Apocrypha* 17 (2006) 9–54.

Bovon, François, and Éric Junod, "Reading the Apocryphal Acts of the Apostles," *Semeia* 38 (1986) 161–71.

Bowersock, Glen W., *Fiction as History: Nero to Julian* (Sather Classical Lectures 58; Berkeley and Los Angeles: University of California Press, 1994).

Bremmer, Jan N., ed., *The Apocryphal Acts of Peter: Magic, Miracles and Gnosticism* (Studies on the Apocryphal Acts of the Apostles 3; Louvain: Peeters, 1998). Conference papers (Rijksuniversiteit Groningen, 1996) and bibliography. (=Bremmer, 1998a)

———, "Aspects of the Acts of Peter: Women, Magic, Place and Date," in idem, *Apocryphal Acts of Peter*, 1–20. (=Bremmer, 1998b)

Brock, Ann Graham, "Political Authority and Cultural Accommodation: Social Diversity in the *Acts of Paul* and the *Acts of Peter*," in Bovon, *Apocryphal Acts of the Apostles*, 145–69.

Burrus, Virginia, *Chastity as Autonomy: Women in the Stories of Apocryphal Acts* (Studies in Women and Religion 23; Lewiston/Queenstown: Edwin Mellen, 1987).

Cartlidge, David, "Transfigurations of Metamorphosis Traditions in the Acts of John, Thomas and Peter," *Semeia* 38 (1986) 56–66.

Cartlidge, David R., and J. Keith Elliott, *Art and the Christian Apocrypha* (London/New York: Routledge, 2001).

Charlesworth, James, "Peter, Acts of," in idem, *The New Testament Apocrypha and Pseudepigrapha: A Guide to Publications with Excurses on Apocalypses* (ATLA Bibliography Series 17; Metuchen, N.J.: Scarecrow, 1987) 309–14.

Czachesz, István, "Who is Deviant? Entering the Story World of *the Acts of Peter*," in Bremmer, *Apocryphal Acts of Peter*, 84–96.

Davies, Stevan L., *The Revolt of the Widows: The Social World of the Apocryphal Acts* (Carbondale: Southern Illinois University Press; London: Feffer & Simons, 1980).

Dinkler, Erich, "Die ersten Petrusdarstellungen: Ein archäologischer Beitrag zur Geschichte des Petrusprimates," *Marburger Jahrbuch für Kunstwissenschaft* 11 (1939) 1–80.

Erbes, C., "Petrus nicht in Rom, sondern in Jerusalem gestorben," *Zeitschrift für Kirchengeschichte* 22 (1901) 1–47, 161–224.

———, "Ursprung und Umfang der Petrusakten," *Zeitschrift für Kirchengeschichte* 32 (1911) 161–85, 353–77, 497–530.

Ficker, Gerhard, "Actus Vercellenses: Einleitung" in Hennecke, ed., *Handbuch* (1924) 226–30.

———, *Die Petrusakten: Beiträge zu ihrem Verständnis* (Leipzig: J. A. Barth, 1903).

———, "Petrusakten," in Hennecke, ed., *Handbuch* (1924) 395–491.

Flamion, J., "Les actes apocryphes de Pierre," *Revue d'histoire ecclésiastique* 9 (1908) 233–54, 465–90; 10 (1909) 5–29, 215–77; 11 (1910) 5–28, 223–56, 447–70, 675–92; 12 (1911) 209–30, 437–50.

Franko, Ivan, " Beiträge aus dem Kirchenslavischen zu den neuetestamentlichen Apokryphen," *Zeitschrift für die neutestamentliche Wissenschaft* 7 (1906) 151–71.

Gallagher, Eugene V., "Conversion and Salvation in the apocryphal Acts of the Apostles," *Second Century: A Journal of Early Christian Studies* 8 (1991) 13–29.

Geerard, Maurice, *Clavis apocryphorum Novi Testamenti* (Corpus Christianorum; Turnhout: Brepols, 1992). See especially "Acta Petri," 101–16.

Halkin, François, "Manuscrits byzantins d'Orchida en Macédoine yougoslave," *Analecta Bollandiana* 80 (1962) 5–21.

Harnack, Adolf von, *Geschichte der altchristlichen Literatur bis Eusebius* (2 vols. in 4 parts; Leipzig: J. C. Hinrichs, 1897; reprinted 1958).

——, *Kritik des Neuen Testaments von einem griechischen Philosophen des 3. Jahrhunderts* (Texte und Untersuchungen zur Geschichte der altchristlichen Literatur 37/4; Leipzig: J. C. Hinrichs, 1911).

——, "Petrus Akten," in idem, *Geschichte der altchristlichen Literatur*, 1. 131–36.

——, "Die Petrusakten," in idem, *Geschichte der altchristlichen Literatur*, 1. 549–60.

——, *Die Pfaff'schen Irenäus-Fragmente als fälschungen Pfaffs Nachgewiesen: Miscellen zu den Apostolischen Vätern, den Acta Pauli, Apelles, dem Muratorischen Fragment, den pseudocyprianischen Schriften und Claudianus Marmertus* (Texte und Untersuchungen zur Geschichte der altchristlichen Literatur 20/3; Leipzig: J. C. Hinrichs, 1900) 100–106.

Hennecke, Edgar, ed., *Handbuch zu den Neutestamentlichen Apokryphen* (Tubingen: J. C. B. Mohr (Siebeck), 1904; 2d. ed., 1924). Detailed notes on text and translation. This volume was published as a companion to the first edition of Hennecke, *Neutestamentliche Apokryphen* (1904; see above).

Hilgenfeld, Adolf, "Die alten Actus Petri," *Zeitschrift für wissenschaftliche Theologie* 46 (1903) 321–41.

Hilhorst, Anton, "The text of the Actus Vercellenses," in Bremmer, *Apocryphal Acts of Peter*, 148–60.

Hock, Ronald, "The Greek Novel," in Aune, *Greco-Roman Literature,* 127–46.

Jacobs, Andrew S., "A Family Affair: Marriage, Class and Ethics in the Apocryphal Acts of the Apostles," *Journal of Early Christian Studies* 7 (1999) 105–38.

Jones, F. Stanley, "Principal Orientations on the Relations Between the Apocryphal Acts (Acts of Paul and Acts of John; Acts of Peter and Acts of John)," in Eugene Lovering, ed., *Society of Biblical Literature 1993 Seminar Papers* (Atlanta: Scholars Press,1993) 485–505.

——, "The Pseudo-Clementines: A History of Research," *Second Century: A Journal of Early Christian Studies* 2 (1982) 1–33, 63–96.

Junod, Eric, "Actes apocryphes et hérésie: le jugement de Photius," in Bovon, *Les actes apocryphes*, 11–24. (=Junod, 1981a)

——, "Créations romanesques et traditions ecclésiastiques dans les actes apocryphes des apôtres: L'Alternative Fiction romanesque—vérité historique: une impasse," *Augustinianum* 23 (1983) 271–85.

——, "Origène, Eusèbe et la tradition sur la répartition des champs de mission des apôtres (Eusèbe, *Histoire ecclésiatique* III,1,1–3)," in Bovon, *Les actes apocryphes*, 233–48. (=Junod, 1981b)

————, "Polymorphie de Dieu sauver," in Julien Ries and , Yvonne Janssens, eds., *Gnosticisme et monde hellénistique: Actes du colloque de Louvain-la-Neuve (11-14 mars 1980)* (Publications de l'Institut orientaliste de Louvain 27; Louvain-la-Neuve: Université catholique de Louvain—Institut orientaliste, 1982) 38–46.

————, "Les vies des philosophes et les actes apocryphes des apôtres poursuivent-ils un dessein similaire?" in Bovon, *Les actes apocryphes*, 209–19. (=Junod, 1981c)

Kaestli, Jean-Daniel, "Les principales orientations de la recherche sur les actes apocryphes des apôtres," in Bovon, *Les actes apocryphes*, 49–67. (=Kaestli, 1981a)

————, "Les scènes d'attribution des champs de mission et de départ de l'apôtre dans les actes apocryphes," in Bovon, *Les actes apocryphes*, 249–64. (=Kaestli, 1981b)

————, "L'utilisation des actes apocryphes des apôtres dans le manichéisme," in Martin Krause, ed., *Gnosis and Gnosticism: Papers Read at the Seventh International Conference on Patristic Studies (Oxford, September 8th-13th, 1975)* (Nag Hammadi Studies 8; Leiden: Brill, 1977) 107–16.

Klauck, Hans-Joseph, *The Apocryphal Acts of the Apostles: An Introduction* (trans. Brian McNeil; Waco, Tex.: Baylor University Press, 2008).

Koester, Helmut, "Formgeschichte/Formkritik II: Neues Testament," in R. Horst, et al., eds., *Theologische Realenzyklopädie* (Berlin/New York: de Gruyter, 1977–) 11. 286–99.

————, "The Miracle-Working Apostles in Conflict with the World: The *Acts of Peter* and the *Acts of Paul*," in idem, *Introduction to the New Testament: History and Literature of Early Christianity* (New York/Berlin: de Gruyter, 1982) 323–28.

————, "One Jesus and Four Primitive Gospels," in idem and James M. Robinson, *Trajectories Through Early Christianity* (Philadelphia: Fortress, 1971) 158–204.

Krause, Martin, "Die Petrusakten in Codex VI von Nag Hammadi" in Martin Krause, ed., *Essays on the Nag Hammadi Texts in Honour of Alexander Böhlig* (Nag Hammadi Studies 3; Leiden: Brill, 1972) 36–58.

Lipsius, Richard Adelbert, "Die Acten des Petrus und des Paulus," in idem, *Die apokryphen Apostelgeschichten und Apostellegenden: Ein Beitrag zur altchristlichen Literaturgeschichte und zu einer zusammenfassenden Darstellung der neutestamentlichen Apokryphen* (Braunschweig: Schwetschke, 1883–90; reprinted Amsterdam: APA-Philo, 1976) 2. 1–423.

————, *Die Quellen der römischen Petrus-Sage kritisch untersucht* (Kiel: Schwer, 1872).

Luttikhuizen, Gerard P., "Simon Magus as a Narrative Figure in the Acts of Peter," in Bremmer, *Apocryphal Acts of Peter*, 39–51.

MacDonald, Dennis R., *The Acts of Andrew* (Early Christian Apocrypha 1; Santa Rosa, Calif.: Polebridge, 2005).

————, *The Acts of Andrew and The Acts of Andrew and Matthias in the City of the Cannibals* (Society of Biblical Literature Texts and Translations 33; Christian Apocrypha Series 1; Atlanta: Scholars Press, 1990).

————, *The Legend and the Apostle: The Battle for Paul in Story and Canon* (Philadelphia: Westminster, 1983).

————, "Which Came First? Intertextual Relationships Among the Apocryphal Acts of the Apostles," *Semeia* 80 (1997) 11–41.

McNeil, Brian, "A Liturgical Source in Acts of Peter 38," *Vigiliae christianae* 33 (1979) 342–46.

Matthews, Christopher R., "The *Acts of Peter* and Luke's Intertextual Heritage," Semeia 80 (1997) 207–22.

———, "Articulate Animals: A Multivalent Motif in the Apocryphal Acts of the Apostles," in Bovon, *Apocryphal Acts of Apostles*, 205–32.

———, "Philip and Simon, Luke and Peter: A Lukan Sequel and Intertextual Success," in Eugene Lovering, ed., *Society of Biblical Literature 1992 Seminar Papers* (Atlanta: Scholars Press, 1992) 133–46.

Molinari, Andrea Lorenzo, *"I Never Knew the Man": The Coptic Act of Peter (Papyrus Berolinensis 802,4) Its Independence from the Apocryphal Acts of Peter, Genre and Origins* (Bibliothèque copte de Nag Hammadi; Section Études 5; Québec: Les Presses de l'Université Laval, 2000).

Nagel, Peter, "Die apokryphen Apostelakten des 2. und 3. Jahrhunderts in der manichä-ischen Literatur: Ein Beitrag zur Frage nach den christlichen Elementen im Manichä-ismus," in Karl-Wolfgang Tröger, ed., *Gnosis und Neues Testament: Studien aus Religions-wissenschaft und Theologie* (Gütersloh: Gütersloher Verlagshaus Mohn, 1973) 149–82.

Nau, François, "Fragment syriaque des Voyages de saint Pierre," *Revue de l'Orient chrétien* 14 (1909) 131–34.

Nissen, Theodor, "Die Petrusakten und ein bardesanitischer Dialog in der Aberkiosvita," *Zeitschrift für die neutestamentliche Wissenschaft* 9 (1908) 190–203; 315–28.

Norelli, Enrico, "Situation des apocryphes pétriniens," *Apocrypha* 2 (1991) 31–83.

O'Connor, Daniel Wm., "Peter in Rome: A Review and Position," in Jacob Neusner, ed., *Christianity, Judaism and Other Greco-Roman Cults: Studies for Morton Smith at Sixty* (Studies in Judaism in Late Antiquity 12; 4 vols.; Leiden: Brill, 1975) 4. 2146–60.

———, *Peter in Rome: The Literary, Liturgical and Archeological Evidence* (New York: Columbia University Press, 1969).

Perkins, Judith B., "The *Acts of Peter* as Intertext: Response to Dennis MacDonald," in Eugene Lovering, ed., *Society of Biblical Literature 1993 Seminar Papers* (Atlanta: Scholars Press, 1993) 627–33.

———, "Healing and Power: The *Acts of Peter*," in idem, *The Suffering Self: Pain and Narrative Representation in the Early Christian Era* (London/New York: Routledge, 1995) 124–41.

———, "Resurrection and Social Perspectives," in idem, *Roman Imperial Identities in the Early Christian Era* (Routledge Monographs in Classical Studies; London/New York: Routledge, 2009) 144–58.

———, "This World or Another? The Intertextuality of the Greek Romances, the Apocryphal Acts and Apuleius' *Metamorphoses*," *Semeia* 80 (1997) 247–60.

Perry, Ben Edwin, *The Ancient Romances: A Literary-Historical Account of Their Origins* (Sather Classical Lectures 37; Berkeley and Los Angeles: University of California Press, 1967).

Pervo, Richard, "Egging on the Chickens: A Cowardly Response to Dennis MacDonald and Then Some," *Semeia* 80 (1997) 43–56.

Plümacher, Eckhard, "Apokryphe Apostelakten," in August Friedrich von Pauly and Georg Wissowa, eds., *Paulys Real-Encyclopädie der classischen Alterthumswissenschaft*: Supplementband 15 (Stuttgart: J. B. Metzler, 1978) 11–70, esp. 19–24.

Poupon, Gérard, "L'accusation de magie dans les actes apocryphes," in Bovon, *Les actes apocryphes,* (1981) 71–93.

————, "Les Actes de Pierre' et leur remaniement," in Hildegard Temporini and Wolfgang Haase, eds., *Aufstieg und Niedergang der römischen Welt* 2:25.6 (Leiden: Brill, 1988) 4363–82.

————, "L'Origine africaine des *Actus Vercellenses*," in Bremmer, *Apocryphal Acts of Peter*, 192–99.

Reardon, Bryan P., *The Form of Greek Romance* (Princeton: Princeton University Press, 1991).

Reitzenstein, Richard, *Hellenistische Wundererzählungen* (2d ed.; Stuttgart, Teubner, 1963; reprinted Darmstadt: Wissenschaftliche Buchgesellschaft, 1974).

Rimoldi, Antonio, "L'apostolo S. Pietro nella letteratura apocrifa dei primi 6 secoli," *Scuola Cattolica* 83 (1955) 196–224.

Rordorf, Willy, "The Relation between the *Acts of Peter* and the *Acts of Paul*: State of the Question," in Bremmer, *Apocryphal Acts of Peter*, 178–91.

Salvatore, Antonio, *Carme apologetico Commodiano* (Torino: Societa editrice internazionale, 1977).

Santos Otero, A. de, *Die handschriftliche Überlieferung der altslavischen Apokryphen,* vol. 1 (Patristische Texte und Studien 20; Berlin/New York: de Gruyter, 1978).

————, "Later Acts of Apostles," in Schneemelcher, ed., *New Testament Apocrypha*, 2. 426–82. (=Santos Otero, 1992a)

————, "The Pseudo-Titus Epistle," in Schneemelcher, ed., *New Testament Apocrypha*, 2. 53–74. (=Santos Otero, 1992b)

Schäferdiek, Knut, "The Manichaean Collection of apocryphal Acts ascribed to Leucius Charinus," in Schneemelcher, *New Testament Apocrypha*, 2. 87–100.

Schmidt, Carl, *Acta Pauli: Aus der Heidelberger Koptischen Papyrushandschrift nr. 1* (2d ed.; Leipzig: Hinrichs, 1905; reprinted Hildesheim: Olms, 1965).

————, *Die alten Petrusakten im Zusammenhang der apokryphen Apostelliteratur, nebst einem neuentdeckten Fragment, untersucht* (Texte und Untersuchungen zur Geschichte der altchristlichen Literatur 24/1; Leipzig: J. C. Hinrichs, 1903).

————, Review of Ficker, *Die Petrusakten* (see above), in *Göttingische gelehrte Anzeigen* 165 (1903): 363–77.

————, "Studien zu den alten Petrusakten," *Zeitschrift für Kirchengeschichte* 43 (1924) 321–48; 45 (1926) 481–515.

————, "Zur Datierung der alten Petrusakten," *Zeitschrift für die neutestamentliche Wissenschaft* 29 (1930) 150–55.

Schmidt, Carl, and Wilhelm Schubart, *PRAXIS PAULOU: Acta Pauli nach dem Papyrus der Hamburger Staats- und Universitätsbibliothek* (Glückstadt and Hamburg: Augustin, 1936).

Schneemelcher, Wilhelm, "Second and Third Century Acts of Apostles: Introduction," in idem, *New Testament Apocrypha*, 2. 75–86. (=Schneemelcher, 1992b)

Smith, Jonathan Z., "Birth Upside Down or Right Side Up?" *History of Religion* 9 (1970) 281–303. Reprinted in idem, *Map is not Territory: Studies in the History of Religions* (Studies in Judaism in Late Antiquity 23; Leiden: Brill, 1978) 147–71.

Söder, Rosa, *Die apokryphen Apostelgeschichten und die romanhafte Literatur der Antike* (Würzburger Studien zur Altertumswissenschaft 3; Stuttgart: Kohlhammer, 1932; reprinted Darmstadt: Wissenschaftliche Buchgesellschaft, 1969).

Sordi, Marta, *The Christians and the Roman Empire* (trans. Annabel Bedini; Norman, Okla.: University of Oklahoma Press, 1986).

Spittler, Janet E., *Animals in the Apocryphal Acts of the Apostles: The Wild Kingdom of Early Christian Literature* (Wissenschaftliche Untersuchungen zum Neuen Testament 2/247; Tübingen: Mohr-Siebeck, 2008). See especially Ch. 6, "Animals in the *Acts of Peter*," 126–55.

Stoops, Robert, "The *Acts of Peter* in Intertextual Context," *Semeia* 80 (1997) 57–86.

———, "Christ as Patron in the *Acts of Peter*," *Semeia* 56 (1991) 143–57.

———, "Departing to Another Place: The *Acts of Peter* and the Canonical Acts of the Apostles," in Eugene Lovering, ed., *Society of Biblical Literature 1994 Seminar Papers* (Atlanta: Scholars Press, 1994) 390–404.

———, "Patronage in the *Acts of Peter*," *Semeia* 38 (1986) 91–100.

———, "Peter, Paul and Priority in the Apocryphal Acts," in Eugene Lovering, ed., *Society of Biblical Literature 1992 Seminar Papers* (Atlanta: Scholars Press, 1992) 225–33.

Stuhlfauth, Georg, *Die apokryphen Petrusgeschichten in der altchristlichen Kunst* (Berlin: de Gruyter, 1925).

Thomas, Christine M., *The Acts of Peter, Gospel Literature, and the Ancient Novel: Rewriting the Past* (Oxford/New York: Oxford University Press, 2003).

———, "Canon and Antitype: The Relationship Between the *Acts of Peter* and the New Testament," *Semeia* 80 (1997) 185–205.

———, "The Prehistory of the Acts of Peter," in Bovon, et al., *Apocryphal Acts of the Apostles*, 39–62.

———, "Revivifying Resurrection Accounts: Techniques of Composition and Rewriting in the *Acts of Peter* cc. 25–28" in Bremmer, *Apocryphal Acts of Peter*, 65–83.

———, "Word and Deed: The *Acts of Peter* and Orality," *Apocrypha* 3 (1992) 125–64.

Tissot, Yves, "Encratisme et actes apocryphes," in Bovon, *Les actes apocryphes*, 109–19.

Turner, C. H., "The Latin Acts of Peter," *Journal of Theological Studies* 32 (1931) 119–33.

Valantasis, Richard, "Narrative Strategies and Synoptic Quandaries: A Response to Dennis MacDonald's Reading of the Acts of Paul and the Acts of Peter," in Eugene Lovering, ed., *Society of Biblical Literature 1992 Seminar Papers* (Atlanta: Scholars Press, 1992) 234–39.

Vielhauer, Philipp, "Die Petrusakten," in idem, *Geschichte der urchristlichen Literatur: Einleitung in das Neue Testament, die Apokryphen und die Apostolischen Väter* (Berlin/New York: de Gruyter, 1975) 696–99.

Von Dobschütz, Ernst, "Der Roman in der altchristlichen Literatur" *Deutsche Rundschau* 111 (1902) 87–106.

Von Haeling, R., "Zwei Fremde in Rom: das Wunderduell des Petrus mit Simon Magus in den Acta Petri," *Römische Quartelschrift für christliche Altertumskunde und Kirchengeschichte* 98 (2003) 47–71.

Westra, L. H., "*Regulae fidei* and Other Creedal Formulations in the *Acts of Peter*," in Bremmer, *Apocryphal Acts of Peter*, 134–47.

Zahn, Theodor, "Die gnostischen Akten des Petrus," in idem,*Geschichte des neutestamentlichen Kanons* (2 vols.; Erlangen/Leipzig: Deichert, 1888–92; reprinted Hildesheim: Olms, 1975) 2. 832–55.

INDEX OF SCRIPTURE

OLD TESTAMENT

OLD TESTAMENT PSEUDEPIGRAPHA

NEW TESTAMENT

APOSTOLIC FATHERS

NEW TESTAMENT APOCRYPHA

OTHER EARLY CHURCH WRITERS

INDEX OF PROPER NAMES

CPSIA information can be obtained
at www.ICGtesting.com
Printed in the USA
BVHW040856200620
581807BV00014B/401